GENES & DISEASE

DIABETES

GENES & DISEASE

GENES & DISEASE

DIABETES

Toney Allman

CHELSEA HOUSE
PUBLISHERS
An imprint of Infobase Publishing

Diabetes

Copyright © 2008 by Infobase Publishing

All rights reserved. No part of this book may be reproduced or utilized in any form or by any means, electronic or mechanical, including photocopying, recording, or by any information storage or retrieval systems, without permission in writing from the publisher. For information contact:

Chelsea House
An imprint of Infobase Publishing
132 West 31st Street
New York NY 10001

Library of Congress Cataloging-in-Publication Data

Allman, Toney.
Diabetes / Toney Allman.
    p. cm. — (Genes and disease)
  Includes bibliographical references and index.
  ISBN 978-0-7910-9585-0 (hardcover)
  1. Diabetes—Genetic aspects. I. Title. II. Series.
  RC660.A572 2008
  616.4'62042—dc22   2008001195

Chelsea House books are available at special discounts when purchased in bulk quantities for businesses, associations, institutions, or sales promotions. Please call our Special Sales Department in New York at (212) 967-8800 or (800) 322-8755.

You can find Chelsea House on the World Wide Web at
http://www.chelseahouse.com

Text design by Annie O'Donnell
Cover design by Ben Peterson

Printed in the United States of America

Bang FOF 10 9 8 7 6 5 4 3 2 1

This book is printed on acid-free paper.

All links and Web addresses were checked and verified to be correct at the time of publication. Because of the dynamic nature of the Web, some addresses and links may have changed since publication and may no longer be valid.

CONTENTS

1

A DIAGNOSIS OF DIABETES

Amanda was 12 years old and always thirsty and always hungry. Even though she ate constantly, she lost 15 pounds in two months. It was the same with fluids. She just could not get enough. She remembers drinking not just glasses of water but gallons of water. She had to constantly go to the bathroom. Finally, her worried parents made a doctor's appointment for her, but before she could get there, she awoke one night dreadfully ill. She had sharp pains in her stomach and was so weak she could not stand. She collapsed on the bathroom floor, exhausted and unable to remain conscious. Her mother rushed her to the doctor, who sent her straight to the hospital. She remained in the hospital for about a week, recovering from her ordeal and learning the diagnosis that would change her life. Amanda had diabetes and that was what had caused all her symptoms.[1]

Kassy was diagnosed with diabetes when she was only 6 years old. Her symptoms were not as obvious as Amanda's. She had stomachaches, but no one knew what was wrong with her. She had been drinking a lot of fluids, but the signal that alerted her parents was that she suddenly started wetting her bed at night. When her mother took her to the hospital emergency room, she fell asleep in the waiting room and wet her chair.[2]

Daniel, a resident of South Africa, was 14 years old when his diabetes was diagnosed. He remembers being so thirsty that he could drink 7 liters of cola a day and still yearn for more. He was not aware of any other symptoms, so the doctor's discovery of diabetes was a shock to him.[3] Daniel's shock was not unusual. Adjusting to a serious disease is not easy for anyone, no matter what age. Even for those who have never heard the word *diabetes* before, shock, distress, and fear are common responses to this diagnosis.

Although most young people learn to adjust relatively soon, the tempo of their lives is changed forever. Diabetes is a lifelong condition and requires medical treatment and management. That most people succeed and live long, active lives is a tribute both to the courage and efforts of individuals and to the medical and scientific knowledge that makes these efforts possible.

TYPE 1 DIABETES

Diabetes is a complex and variable condition that can affect almost every organ in the body. To make matters even more complicated, it is not even one disease. Diabetes is actually several diseases with different causes, different ages of onset, and different treatment requirements. Amanda, Daniel, and Kassy have what is known as **type 1 diabetes**. According to the United States Centers for Disease Control (CDC), each year, more than 13,000 young people are diagnosed with type 1 diabetes. It usually begins in childhood, adolescence, or young adulthood. It has a rapid onset and can make the affected person very sick very quickly. Actress Halle Berry, for example, suddenly collapsed while working on a television sitcom one day in 1989 at the age of 21. She was rushed to the hospital in a diabetic coma. She had little

FIGURE 1.1   Actress Halle Berry, winner of the 2002 Oscar for Best Actress, has type 1 diabetes. She is an active volunteer for the Juvenile Diabetes Association.

warning that she was sick, except for feeling very tired and wanting to lie down that day.[4]

Berry's coma was a symptom of uncontrolled type 1 diabetes. Other symptoms are thirst, unusual hunger, weight loss, frequent urination, and tiredness. Sickness, stomach pain, blurred vision, weakness, and dizziness may also occur in type 1 diabetes. All these symptoms arise because the sick person's pancreas has stopped working effectively.

WHAT'S HAPPENING INSIDE THE BODY

The **pancreas** is an organ located behind the stomach. This fish-shaped organ has two main functions. First, it helps the body to digest food by producing enzymes. The enzymes are chemicals that help the intestine to break down food. Most importantly, the pancreas also manufactures **insulin** so that the body can use the food that is eaten. Insulin is a **hormone**, a chemical made by one part of the body that controls the function of another part of the body. Insulin is critical to life. It is the key that enables the body to use the food that is its fuel.

When food is eaten and digested, the nutrients are turned into a special kind of sugar called **glucose**. Glucose is the food and energy for all the **cells** that make up bodies. Human bodies are made of trillions of microscopic cells. Each cell is a tiny factory enclosed in a membrane, somewhat like a balloon. Cells in the lungs breathe; cells in the heart beat; cells in the eyes gather light. Every cell does the work of some part of the body, and every cell requires glucose as energy in order to do its job.

The Insulin Glucose System

Glucose is carried throughout the body by the bloodstream. It is delivered to the cells of the body by the blood, but it

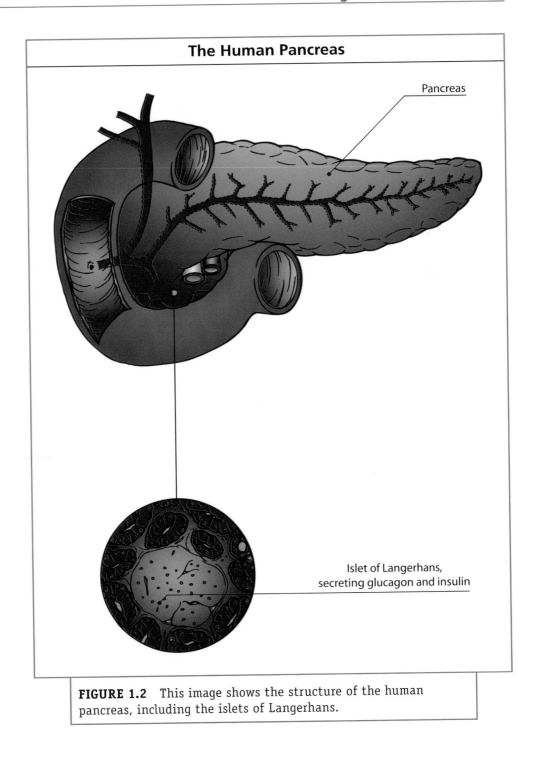

The Human Pancreas

Pancreas

Islet of Langerhans,
secreting glucagon and insulin

FIGURE 1.2 This image shows the structure of the human
pancreas, including the islets of Langerhans.

cannot enter the cells without the help of insulin. Every time food is eaten, glucose enters the blood. The pancreas responds to the presence of glucose by making and sending out insulin. The insulin travels to the cells. Substances called **insulin receptors**, which are on the surfaces of cells, bind together with the insulin, and this unlocks the cell's door to admit the glucose. The cells use the glucose for the energy they need to do their work. Without glucose, cells would starve and die. Without insulin, however, cells cannot get glucose. Without insulin, the body's cells would, in effect, starve to death.

This insulin and glucose system works perfectly in most bodies to keep the cells healthy. The more food that is eaten and digested, the more insulin is made by the pancreas. If no food is eaten, the pancreas turns off insulin production

DIABETES AND THE HALL OF FAMER

Jackie Robinson was the first African American to play major league baseball. He began in 1947 with the Brooklyn Dodgers. Despite being a major star, he faced terrible prejudice and bigotry, which he handled calmly and gracefully. He became a civil rights leader and a hero to many millions. Racism, however, was not the only challenge Robinson had to face. In 1957, shortly after he retired from baseball, he was diagnosed with type 2 diabetes. The disease eventually disabled him and shortened his life during a time when treatments were not as successful as they are today. Robinson's hair turned white, his legs were numb and crippled, he had high blood pressure, and he was almost completely blind before a heart attack killed him in 1972 at the age of only 53.

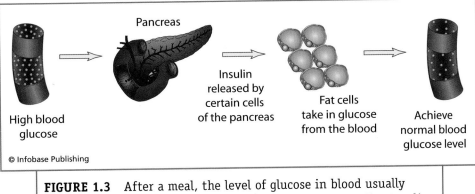

Pancreas

Insulin released by certain cells of the pancreas

Fat cells take in glucose from the blood

High blood glucose

Achieve normal blood glucose level

© Infobase Publishing

FIGURE 1.3 After a meal, the level of glucose in blood usually rises. In response, beta cells in the pancreas release insulin. Insulin stimulates body cells, such as fat cells and muscle cells, to take up the glucose to be used for energy or storage. As a result, glucose levels in the blood return to normal.

because glucose in the blood is low. A healthy pancreas never allows too much or too little glucose to exist in the blood. Just enough insulin is produced so that the glucose in the blood can be used by the cells. If extra glucose is available (for instance, if a person ate a huge meal), the pancreas directs fat cells and the liver to store it for future use. That way, if a person is doing a lot of work and has not eaten enough, glucose is available to give the muscles the extra energy they need. Insulin keeps the blood glucose level in balance all the time. It ensures that cells never lack energy.

Beta Cells

Insulin is made in special areas of the pancreas called islets of Langerhans. These areas are named after Paul Langerhans, the German scientist who discovered them. Two of the most important kinds of cells in the islets of Langerhans are alpha cells and **beta cells**. Both help the body to control and use its blood sugar. Alpha cells make a hormone called glucagon. This hormone raises blood sugar if it gets too low. Beta cells produce insulin. Insulin lowers blood sugar by directing cells to use it or store it.

People with type 1 diabetes have a pancreas that cannot make enough insulin because beta cells have been destroyed. If 80% of beta cells die, type 1 diabetes develops, and the pancreas produces either very little or no insulin. Body cells cannot get enough glucose to stay healthy or even survive. Glucose in the blood rises higher and higher without ever entering the cells. This is what makes a person with type 1 diabetes so sick. A person with untreated diabetes is, in a sense, "starving in the midst of plenty," because the cells are starving no matter how much food the person eats.

High blood sugar causes serious problems, too. Almost every organ in the body is damaged by high levels of glucose in the blood. Kidneys work very hard to filter out the extra sugar in the blood. This makes people have to urinate often and can damage the kidneys, too, as they work overtime to try to clean the blood. Muscles with too little glucose are worn out and tired. In a desperate effort to feed the cells, fat and muscle cells are broken down for the energy they contain. As the body breaks down, the person loses weight. If the diabetes is not treated, every organ in the body will die. A person with type 1 diabetes must get insulin in some way if he or she is to survive.

When type 1 diabetes is diagnosed, doctors prescribe insulin injections. These shots provide the insulin that the pancreas is no longer producing. For the rest of their lives, people with diabetes carefully balance the insulin they inject, the food they eat, and the exercise they get so that they can keep their bodies healthy. Once this is achieved, most can live long, active lives.

TYPE 2 DIABETES

Not everyone with diabetes needs insulin shots. As a matter of fact, according to the CDC, 90% to 95% of people with diabetes do not. These people have a different kind of diabetes, known as **type 2 diabetes**. Type 2 diabetes is also a disease of high blood glucose, but it differs from type 1 in several important ways. People diagnosed with type 1 are usually underweight, for example, while those with type 2 tend to be overweight and physically inactive. Also, type 2 most often appears in people older than 40 years (although it increasingly is found in younger people). It tends to come on much more slowly than type 1, and does not make people so sick so fast. When it does strike, though, it can be just as serious.

Danielle Kazista was a 39-year-old mother of two. For about a year, she just felt "out of sorts." Month after month, she caught different minor illnesses. She had stomach upsets and headaches frequently. She was always tired and wanted to sleep a lot. Then one day, while she was on a vacation cruise, she fainted after eating a particularly rich, sugary meal. Once she got home, she felt even more run down. She had cramps and diarrhea. She slept almost all the time, just waking up to go to the bathroom. Finally, her doctor tested her blood and urine. He discovered that she had type 2 diabetes. The glucose in her blood was very high. Her urine showed that her kidneys were working so hard to filter out the glucose in her blood that they were not keeping up. Kazista was frightened and could not believe what she was hearing. She left the doctor's office in despair and cried all the way home.[5]

Singer Patti LaBelle found out about her type 2 diabetes in an even more dramatic way. In 1994, when she was 50 years old, LaBelle was feeling overworked and exhausted.

She thought she just needed a break from touring, but she kept pushing herself. Then one night at a concert, she passed out on stage. She was rushed to a hospital, where doctors told her she had collapsed because of type 2 diabetes. LaBelle was shocked and feared she was going to die. LaBelle's blood glucose was very high, but she had not even known she was sick.[6]

High Blood Sugar

Without diagnosis and treatment, people can die from type 2 diabetes and high blood sugar. Just like people with type 1 diabetes, people with type 2 diabetes have too much glucose in their blood. Blood glucose is measured in milligrams as a ratio of the amount in a deciliter of blood. (A deciliter is a tenth of a liter, or about 3 ounces.) Normal **blood glucose levels** are between 60 and 100 milligrams per deciliter. That ratio is usually written 60–100 mg/dl. A milligram is not much; it is one-thousandth of a gram, which is only about three-thousandths of a teaspoon of sugar. Yet this tiny amount of glucose is critical to the health of every cell in the body, and it must stay in just the right range.

People with a glucose level above 125 mg/dl are considered to have diabetes. In these people, the amount of sugar in the blood can skyrocket. Kazista, for example, had a blood glucose reading of 600 mg/dl at the time of her diagnosis. Some people with type 1 diabetes can have blood glucose levels of 1200 mg/dl or more. Both type 1 and type 2 cause high blood glucose levels, but for different reasons. In type 1, glucose levels are very high because the pancreas is not producing insulin. In type 2, the pancreas still produces insulin—sometimes a lot of it—but that insulin is not unlocking the cells. The cells are resistant to the insulin, and it is hard for glucose to get inside the cells. This is called **insulin resistance**, and it means that cells are either

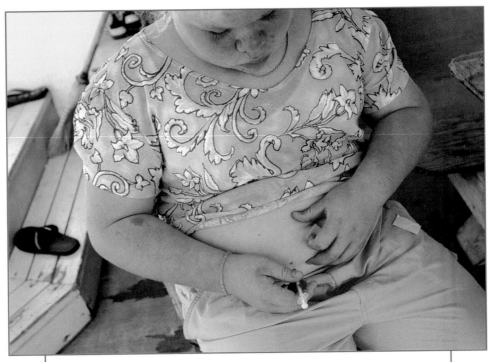

FIGURE 1.4   This 12-year-old girl with type 2 diabetes is giving herself an insulin injection in her abdomen.

malnourished or starved as sugar levels in the blood rise higher and higher. In response, the pancreas works harder and harder, pumping out more and more insulin and trying to lower glucose levels. As time goes on, beta cells may burn out completely from this overwork, and therefore less and less insulin can be made. If too many beta cells die, a person with type 2 diabetes may require insulin shots.

Complications

Even when medically treated, many people with type 2 diabetes may have glucose levels in the 200-mg/dl range for many years. The longer this situation lasts, the more damage occurs to body organs. These secondary complications make type 2 diabetes very dangerous. Kidneys can fail; eyes and vision can be damaged; blood pressure can rise; harmful fats in the blood like cholesterol and triglycerides can increase; heart disease becomes more common; nerve damage can occur; and feet can develop sores and ulcers and become so damaged that they have to be amputated. Many older people who have had type 2 for years suffer from these complications. In 2005, for example, the CDC estimated that people with diabetes died of heart disease two to four times more often than people without diabetes. In 2002, the CDC noted that 82,000 people with diabetes required foot or leg amputations. That is why type 2 is the sixth leading cause of death in the United States and is also a leading cause of disabilities. Kazista's mother and brother, for example, both died of heart disease caused by diabetes. LaBelle's aunt and grandmother died of the disease, and her mother had both legs amputated from diabetes complications.

TYPE 2 DIABETES IN CHILDREN

Usually adults—particularly those who are overweight and get little exercise—are more at risk for type 2 diabetes. However, this is not always the case. Both Kazista and LaBelle were of normal weight and active when their diabetes was diagnosed. Type 2 diabetes is becoming more frequent in younger people, too. Nathan Carter, a resident of Kentucky, was only 14 years old when he began to feel tired all the time and could not get enough to drink. When he got too tired to want to go to school, his mother took him to the doctor. The doctor discovered his blood sugar was very high and diagnosed Nathan with type 2 diabetes.[7] The number of young people who have been diagnosed with diabetes has increased dramatically in the last decade. This worries medical experts. They believe the increase has been caused by overweight; high-fat, sugary diets and lack of exercise in young people. The only way to stop the dramatic rise in type 2 diabetes in the young is to change this lifestyle. Usually, complications occur after decades of living with diabetes, and that means when people are elderly. Diabetes is becoming a national and even global epidemic, however, and experts believe if diabetes continues to be diagnosed at younger ages, the age at which complications occur will likewise drop in the future.

Diabetes, whether type 1 or type 2, is a serious, lifelong disease. Fortunately, good treatments are available today, and most people can achieve good health. Living with

THE THIRD MAJOR KIND OF DIABETES

Scientists and doctors today recognize a third major type of diabetes. It is called gestational diabetes. This kind of diabetes develops only when a woman is pregnant, and disappears after she has given birth. Gestational diabetes brings on high blood sugar in a woman who has never had the problem before. About 135,000 pregnant women develop gestational diabetes every year. Just as with type 1 and type 2, no one is sure what causes gestational diabetes, but scientists have identified some risk factors. Women who have type 2 diabetes in their families, are overweight before getting pregnant, or are older than 25 appear to have a greater chance of getting diabetes during pregnancy than others. It is also more common in Native Americans, African Americans, and Pacific Island peoples. Even though gestational diabetes usually goes away once the baby is born, doctors are concerned about it. If it is not treated, it can be dangerous for the baby, and it signals a risk for the mother to develop type 2 diabetes later in life.

diabetes, however, is complicated and life-changing. This volume focuses on the genetic basis of diabetes—what scientists currently know and what they hope to learn in the near future about the relationship between diabetes and our genes. The discussion begins in Chapter 2 with how diabetes was discovered and how it is currently treated. Chapter 3 explores how genes and DNA work. Genetic engineering of human insulin, which has transformed treatment, is described in Chapter 4. The following two chapters look at the genetic basis of type 1 and type 2 diabetes, and Chapter 7 explores gene therapy for diabetes, a promising new area of research. Chapter 8 examines stem cell research and how it may someday lead to a cure for diabetes. That cure has been a long time coming. People have suffered with diabetes for thousands of years, and for most of that time, science had few answers.

2

TREATING DIABETES

Today, young people like Daniel, Kassy, and Amanda are leading normal, healthy lives. Halle Berry and Patti Labelle are active entertainers, and Danielle Kazista is a grandmother of six who is successfully controlling her diabetes. Medical science enables most people with diabetes to lower their blood sugars and be healthy. The treatment of diabetes, however, can be difficult, especially over the long term. Modern science continues to search for better treatment methods.

Normalizing blood sugar is the major goal of all diabetes treatment. Nowadays, good control of blood sugar keeps people with diabetes healthy, but this was not always the case. Throughout most of human history, doctors had no way to alter blood sugar levels. Diabetes has been around since ancient times, and until the twentieth century, it was an invariably fatal disease.

ANCIENT KNOWLEDGE OF DIABETES

More than 3,500 years ago, Egyptian physicians described a disease marked by excessive urination. Ancient Hindu physicians often diagnosed diabetes because ants and flies were attracted to the urine of those affected. They also described the terrible thirst of people with the disease and noted how the patient wasted away until succumbing to death.

Physicians in ancient Greece described diabetes in detail and gave the world its name. Aretaeus and Galen were two Greek physicians who listed symptoms of diabetes. They noted the excessive thirst and urination and said that flesh melted into nothingness as patients starved to death. Aretaeus, who lived about 2,000 years ago, described the body of the diabetic patient as a "siphon;" water poured in and out of the body as if it were a hose. The word *diabetes* is based on the Greek word for "siphon." Aretaeus described the "melting down of the flesh and limbs into urine," and Galen called the disease "diarrhea of the urine."[8] The Greek physicians tasted the patient's urine to diagnose diabetes

PHONY TREATMENTS

Living with diabetes can be so hard that many people search for miracle cures. Fraudulent products directed at people with diabetes are common on the Internet. Some unscrupulous people sell herbs or vitamins that claim to cure diabetes and end the need for insulin and oral medications. Others sell diet plan books that claim to reverse autoimmune attacks, complete with patient testimonials. New "scientific breakthroughs" are advertised via email. Reputable doctors and scientists try to protect people from wasting money on devices and unproven treatments. Some of them can even be dangerous and cause hypoglycemia or other sicknesses. As many scientists point out, if any product had been developed that cures diabetes, the discoverer would be world famous and would have won a Nobel Prize.

and described it as being sweet. Much later, in the seventeenth century, the term *mellitus*—from the Greek word for "honey"—was added to the disease's name. Diabetes mellitus became the formal name for the disorder.

Gathering Knowledge About Diabetes

As the centuries passed, healers in all parts of the world became adept at diagnosing diabetes, but they could not treat it. Until the twentieth century, diabetes remained a fatal disease. After diagnosis, adults might live for several years, but children who developed the disease were often dead within weeks.

By the early 1900s, scientists knew that something in the islets of Langerhans of the pancreas was related to diabetes. They knew that a lack of some substance caused a person with diabetes to be unable to use food. They knew that removing pancreases from dogs led to diabetes and death. What they did not know was what to do about it.

Starvation Treatment

About 1920, Frederick Allen, an American physician, developed the first treatment that prolonged life for people with diabetes. The treatment, however, was rather extreme. Allen's treatment was a rigid starvation diet. His goal was to rid the urine of sugar. The sugar was an indication that the body could not process the food that was eaten, and that was why it was eliminated through the urine. Therefore, Allen reasoned, the patient needed a treatment that would rest the body by giving it less food to process. People with diabetes were allowed to eat only about 400–600 calories a day. They were fed these calories mostly from fats, while carbohydrates and sugar were severely restricted. The treatment actually helped people who had type 2 diabetes. The restriction of sugar and starches helped their bodies to recover, if only for a few years. People with type 1 diabetes, however, suffered through additional months of misery. Since doctors and scientists did not know there were

MODY

Some unusual kinds of diabetes have a simple genetic cause, like Huntington's disease or cystic fibrosis. Aaron Snyder has one of these rare forms. His pancreas produces only about half the normal amount of insulin. Before Snyder was diagnosed, he constantly craved sugar. He was hungry and thirsty much of the time and was exhausted no matter how much he rested or slept. When Snyder's diabetes was diagnosed, he was 22 years old. He was not overweight but had very high blood glucose levels. The doctor thought Snyder had type 2 diabetes, but he does not. After years of misdiagnosis, doctors discovered that Snyder had MODY, which is short for "mature onset diabetes of the young." So did his great-grandmother, his grandfather, and his mother. Snyder works hard with diet and exercise to keep his blood sugar in normal ranges. So far, it has worked, but he fears that someday he will need insulin.

MODY is different from other forms of diabetes. It is not caused by multiple genes or affected by environmental triggers. It is caused by just one dominant, mutated gene and is passed from generation to generation. Each child of a person with MODY has a 50% chance of inheriting the MODY gene and developing diabetes. Since MODY's mode of transmission is easy to understand, genetic scientists are very interested in the disease, even though only 3 to 5% of people with diabetes have MODY genes. Scientists have discovered six different genes with errors in them that can cause MODY.

different forms of diabetes, they had no way of knowing who might be helped by the starvation treatment. Besides, Allen's treatment was the only known way to prolong life, even a little, for anyone with diabetes.

In 1919, Elizabeth Hughes, the daughter of New York's governor Charles Evans Hughes, was diagnosed with diabetes. She was 11 years old and almost 5 feet tall but weighed only 75 pounds. Despite her emaciated condition, Allen began to starve her. He hoped to prolong her life by allowing her to eat as little as possible, but he knew he could give her only another couple of years at most. Some days, Elizabeth was allowed no food at all. Other days, she might be given a little meat, lettuce, milk, or bran. Some people on diets like Elizabeth's got so desperate that they ate things like toothpaste and birdseed. Elizabeth did her best to follow doctor's orders. Her weight dropped to just 52 pounds, but at age 13, she was still alive. It was 1921, and Elizabeth, though she could not know it, was about to be rescued. She just had to hang on a little longer.[9]

THE DISCOVERY OF INSULIN

In Canada, Frederick Banting and Charles Best were determined to find the chemical in the pancreas that was so essential for life. In a lab in the University of Toronto under the direction of John Macleod, Banting and Best experimented with dogs. They removed the pancreases from some of the dogs, who were then injected with extracts from the islets of Langerhans from other dogs. The dogs lived. Excited by this success, they acquired cattle pancreases from slaughterhouses and feverishly worked to extract and purify the critical substance. Finally, they succeeded. When the chemical from cattle pancreases was

FIGURE 2.1 Charles Best and Frederick Banting discovered insulin with the help of dogs. The dog in this photograph was the first dog to be kept alive by insulin.

given to dogs that lacked a pancreas, the dogs survived. It was January 1922, and the scientists had discovered and isolated insulin.

Back from the Dead

Banting's team was ready to try the insulin treatment on a human patient. They chose Leonard Thompson, a 14-year-old boy dying of diabetes in a Toronto hospital. He weighed 64 pounds. The insulin that Banting and Best brought to him was not very pure. When it was injected into Leonard, he developed sores around the injection site. The boy got sicker, but not before doctors noticed that his blood sugar had dropped temporarily. James Collip, a scientist on the team, spent about six weeks figuring out a way to improve and refine the insulin. The team returned to Leonard's bedside and injected him with purified insulin. Within 24 hours, Leonard's blood sugar levels dropped from 520 mg/dl to 120 mg/dl. With regular injections, he gained weight and grew healthy. The news spread throughout the medical world with lightning speed: Insulin could save the lives of people with diabetes.[10]

Allen heard about the discovery and immediately went to Toronto to get some of the insulin for his patients. The Canadian team gave Allen some insulin, but there was not enough for everyone. Purifying insulin was difficult and slow in these early days. Elizabeth Hughes's father could not wait. Elizabeth's weight was down to 45 pounds. Charles Hughes took her directly to Toronto, where Banting began insulin treatment. From the very first injection, Elizabeth's urine was free of sugar. Within two weeks, she was eating 2,200 calories a day. By the end of that year, she weighed 105 pounds and was at home with her family, healthy and happy. All it took was continuing her insulin shots twice a day. Insulin saved Elizabeth and thousands of others like her. As she wrote to her mother soon after the treatment started, "It is simply too wonderful for words."[11]

MODERN KNOWLEDGE OF DIABETES

Insulin seemed like a miracle. Yet as time went on, and people with diabetes lived for years instead of dying quickly, scientists realized that it was not enough. They began to see the long-term complications that resulted from diabetes. They found that some people with diabetes had very different problems than others. They discovered that lives were shortened by these problems and that they needed a better understanding of how diabetes affected bodies. In 1959, scientists recognized that there was more than one kind of diabetes. With more research, they have come to understand what goes wrong in the body that causes diabetes.

Today, scientists know that type 1 is an **autoimmune** disease. This means that the body's immune system mistakenly attacks a part of itself. Normally, the **immune system** is the body's defense. It is a complex system of many components, such as T cells and macrophages, which attack and destroy invaders. Most of these defenders circulate in the blood. Whenever an invader is detected, the immune system battles the germ or infection. Once the immune system has successfully fought off a disease, it produces **antibodies** to that disease. Antibodies are proteins made by the body that recognize foreign invaders and launch an attack on them. If the disease ever recurs, the antibodies immediately recognize the invader. Sometimes, however, this elegant system goes awry. The parts of the immune system that distinguish between "self" and "nonself" do not work correctly. (The term *auto-* means "self".) In an autoimmune disease, the immune system fails to recognize certain cells as part of the

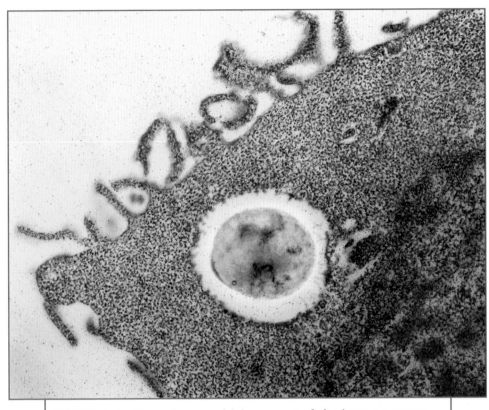

FIGURE 2.2 Macrophages, which are part of the immune system, attack an invading cell.

body and attacks them, just as if those cells were a foreign invader. This is what happens in type 1 diabetes. Antibodies mistakenly identify beta cells as nonself, and the immune system destroys them.

Many scientists believe that this attack is triggered by a common virus, perhaps similar to the cold or flu virus. It causes no problems in most people, but in some, it may lead to an autoimmune attack. In the case of type 1 diabetes, scientists speculate that something in the structure of the virus is similar to some feature of the beta cells. Whatever the reason, in type 1 diabetics, most of the beta cells are destroyed and can no longer produce insulin. Diabetes is the result.

Type 2 diabetes is not an autoimmune disease. It generally occurs in overweight, physically inactive people who eat a diet high in fat and sugar. It also tends to run in families. People with family members who have type 2 diabetes are much more likely to get diabetes themselves. Yet most people who are obese or eat a poor diet do not get diabetes. Something in a vulnerable person's body causes insulin resistance to develop. The insulin resistance eventually leads to diabetes.

MODERN TREATMENTS OF DIABETES

Doctors cannot yet stop an immune system attack or reverse a tendency to insulin resistance. Instead, they control diabetes by treating its symptoms. Many different kinds of drugs are available now to help people with diabetes, but insulin is still the biggest lifesaver.

Insulin has been vastly improved since the days of Banting and Best. Today, scientists know that two shots a day of the same amount of insulin is not a recipe for long-term health for everyone. The body automatically adjusts the amount of insulin according to the amount of food eaten, the type of food eaten, the level of exercise, and even the amount of stress or worry a person suffers. All these triggers affect how much insulin is required to keep blood sugar levels stable. Today, insulin injections are adjusted to individual needs. People on insulin must be careful not to skip meals. They keep fast-acting foods like sugar and carbohydrates to a minimum. They test their blood levels after exercise and inject more insulin if it is needed. They perform a constant balancing act in order to normalize glucose levels as much as possible. They know that long-term complications can arise due to many years of fluctuating, or varying, glucose levels.

Glucose levels that are too high are bad for body organs and can shorten life or lead to disabilities. A high level of glucose in the blood is called **hyperglycemia**. A glucose level that is too low can be very dangerous, too. This is called **hypoglycemia** and can happen when too much insulin is in the bloodstream. A person with hypoglycemia can quickly become shaky or disoriented, lose consciousness, or even die. Most people who inject insulin carry sugar pills or sweets with them at all times in case they make a mistake, inject too much insulin, and end up with too little sugar in their blood. This emergency situation is the only time sugar is good for a person with diabetes.

USING INSULIN TODAY

Life with diabetes is much more complicated than just injecting insulin and forgetting the problem. People with diabetes must continually be aware of whether the amount of sugar in their blood is within a healthy range. Glucose meters enable people to easily check their sugar levels. They can check their blood glucose by pricking a finger to get a drop of blood. The blood is transferred to a testing strip that is inserted into the meter. Within seconds, the meter gives a reading of the sugar level. If the sugar level is too high, the right amount of insulin can be injected so as to lower glucose levels and bring them into the normal range. If glucose levels are too low, no insulin is injected, and instead, something sweet can be eaten to bring the sugar levels up to normal.

Different kinds of insulin are available now, too, to help people keep sugar levels normal. There is fast-acting insulin for times when people need to get insulin working quickly. There is slow-acting insulin that works on glucose levels for

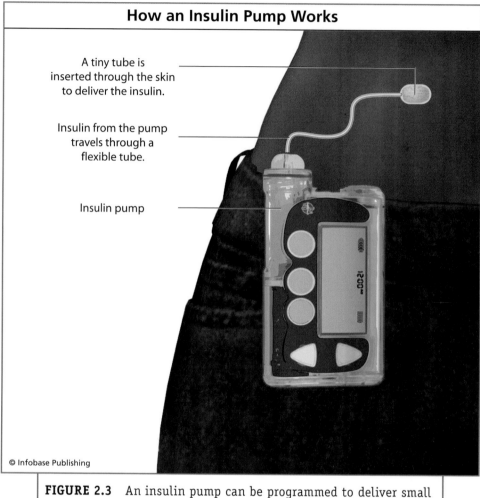

How an Insulin Pump Works

A tiny tube is inserted through the skin to deliver the insulin.

Insulin from the pump travels through a flexible tube.

Insulin pump

FIGURE 2.3 An insulin pump can be programmed to deliver small amounts of insulin into the body at regular intervals.

hours at a time. There are also new ways of getting insulin into the body. Some people wear insulin pumps. These devices are connected to the body with a needle and can take constant measurements of glucose levels. They can deliver insulin at any time. These pumps even have built-in alarms that warn diabetics when glucose levels have become dangerously high or low. A hope for the future is to combine meters with pumps to automatically inject insulin whenever it is needed. This would come close to the body's own insulin glucose system.

Some people are also experimenting with inhaled insulin. This fine, powdered form of insulin can be breathed in. Inhaled insulin is quite new and not yet used by many people. Scientists are not yet certain that it is as safe and effective as insulin injections.

MEDICINES FOR TYPE 2

People with type 2 diabetes often use drugs besides insulin to control their diabetes. Fewer than half of all people with type 2 need insulin. Most work hard to change their diet and lose weight so as to reduce insulin resistance. A diet that is healthy and low in simple carbohydrates and sugars can often improve type 2 diabetes. This means no high-fat or sugary snacks, no fast foods, and plenty of whole grains and vegetables. Combined with exercise, such a diet may be all that a person needs to lose weight and keep type 2 diabetes under control. These lifestyle changes can be very difficult to make, however, and often do not continue to control glucose levels as time passes. Many people with type 2 diabetes need medicines, either oral or injected, to get their blood glucose levels to a normal range. Some medicines help the pancreas to produce more insulin. Other medicines work by lowering the insulin resistance of the body's cells. Still others lower the excess amount of insulin in the blood put out by overworked beta cells. This prevents the liver from releasing stored glucose and helps to stop the vicious cycle that burns out beta cells.

All diabetes medicines are lifesavers, but all have problems, too. Many, including insulin, make people feel very hungry, making it extremely hard to diet. Most cause weight gain. Like injected insulin, these medicines work all the time, even when they are not needed. There is no fine-tuned, balanced system that keeps blood glucose as stable as a healthy pancreas does naturally. Often, people with type 2 struggle to control their diabetes.

Danielle Kazista, for example, spent about 20 years failing to get her diabetes under control. She took oral medicines that made her hungry and encouraged her body to put on weight. Doctors tried insulin, but it also made her crave sweets. Even though she improved as each new medicine was started, over time, her blood sugar would rise. She gained 60 pounds as her hunger grew out of control, and her diabetes got worse. In 2005, Kazista began a new drug called Byetta™. It was a different kind of drug that encouraged Kazista's pancreas to make insulin only when it was needed, instead of all the time. Like many people who tried this medicine, Kazista did well. Her blood sugars became stable, and she lost about 45 pounds over a period of a year and a half.[12]

Scientists have long been aware that diabetes drugs are far from perfect. Many people do not maintain glucose control even with several medicines. Scientists continue to work on devising new medicines, such as Byetta™, to help bodies improve the glucose insulin system.

A TREATMENT, NOT A CURE

Even though medicines for diabetes keep getting better, they are only a treatment, not cure, for the disease. A cure for diabetes depends on scientists being able to answer some major questions. For example, why do some people's immune systems attack their own beta cells? Why do people develop insulin resistance? Is it possible for the pancreas to grow new beta cells? Are people born with a vulnerability to diabetes? The only way to answer these and other questions is to know exactly what is happening inside cells. That is where scientists have to go if they are to prevent or cure diabetes.

3

GENES AND DNA

The answer to the puzzle of diabetes hides inside almost every cell in the body. Each cell does its job because it is equipped with the exact instructions that direct it to make certain proteins. Proteins are the substances that do the work in the body's cells. If scientists could crack that instructional code, they would know what is wrong inside malfunctioning cells. With that knowledge, they might even be able to fix the problem and cure diseases such as diabetes.

PROTEIN FACTORIES

Cells are the building blocks of all life. They are living things that require oxygen, take in glucose for energy, manufacture proteins, and perform all the functions that keep bodies alive and healthy. In each body organ, billions of cells work together, doing their particular jobs as parts of an elegantly organized system. A cell is an intricate factory. Inside the balloon of its membrane is the jelly-like substance called **cytoplasm**. Within the cytoplasm are tiny cell organs, called **organelles**. Cells know what to do because of the messages that travel on an organelle called the **endoplasmic reticulum**. It is a network of tubes and sacs that carries messages to and from the cell's **nucleus**. The nucleus contains spiraled coils of **DNA (deoxyribonucleic acid)**. DNA is the material that carries the genetic instructions for making every living thing.

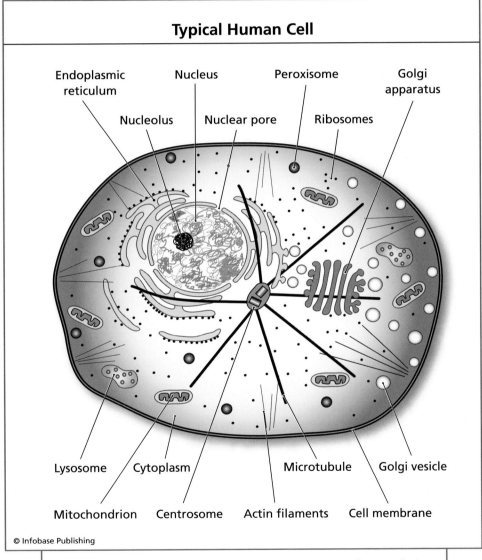

Typical Human Cell

Endoplasmic reticulum

Nucleus

Peroxisome

Golgi apparatus

Nucleolus

Nuclear pore

Ribosomes

Lysosome

Cytoplasm

Microtubule

Golgi vesicle

Mitochondrion

Centrosome

Actin filaments

Cell membrane

FIGURE 3.1 A cell is an intricate factory with a nucleus and tiny organs called organelles.

In humans, the DNA in the nucleus is arranged into 23 pairs of **chromosomes**. Each chromosome is made up of thousands of **genes**. Genes are strings of DNA that are specific units of inheritance. Each codes for a specific protein. Genes determine how cells will operate. Chromosomes are like recipes, and each gene is like an ingredient. The instructions for the ingredients are spelled out by the DNA chemical alphabet. It writes the set of rules that tells the cells how to function.

The DNA alphabet is made up of four chemical letters. They are A (which stands for the chemical called adenine), T (the chemical thymine), G (the chemical guanine), and C (the chemical cytosine). Two strands of DNA are arranged in a twisted, spiraling ladder. At each rung on the ladder, A joins only with T to make a base or rung of the ladder, and C links with G. Each rung is called a base pair, and there are about 3 billion base pairs like this in the DNA ladder. Genes are specific strings of these base pairs that code for a protein. The code directs the cell to make its special protein. A beta cell's DNA, for example, directs it to produce insulin.

RECEIVING THE DNA INSTRUCTIONS

DNA instructions in the nucleus are just the carriers of information. They do not act on the cell directly or even provide it with instructions. This is the job of **RNA (ribonucleic acid)**. RNA is the cell's messenger and transfer system. It is how the cell determines what it is supposed to do. Unlike DNA, RNA consists of only one strand. It has a four-letter chemical alphabet, but instead of a T, it has a U (the chemical uracil). Its other letters are the same. There are many types of RNA, each with a different function in the cell. A type of RNA called **messenger RNA** enters the cell's

Double Helix

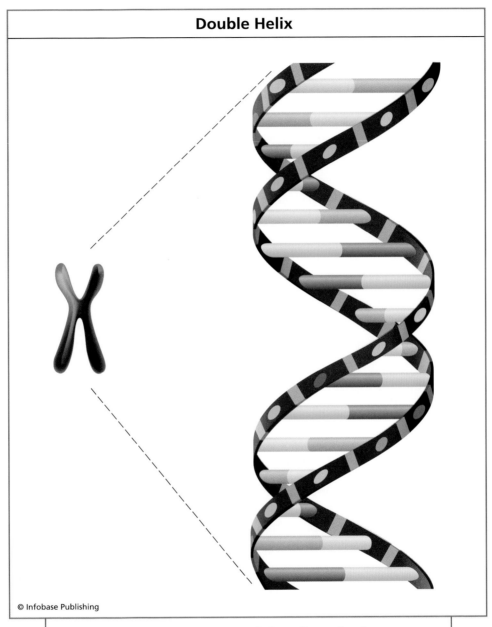

FIGURE 3.2 Within the nucleus of the cell are the chromosomes, which are coiled spirals of DNA. A gene is a specific string of DNA on the chromosome that codes for a unit of inheritance.

nucleus, and the DNA ladder unzips, leaving half a ladder that can pair with the RNA–A to U, T to A, G to C, and C to G. In this way, messenger RNA copies the DNA instructions. Then it travels along the endoplasmic reticulum to the **ribosomes**.

Ribosomes are the organelles that actually make cell proteins. They hold another kind of RNA called **transfer RNA (tRNA)**. Transfer RNA reads the message brought in by messenger RNA. It does this in a very specific way—in triplets, or groups of three. Its molecules are chemical prongs that fit into the strand of messenger RNA.

USING THE CODE

Henry Gee, a genetic scientist, explains that transfer RNA is like a three-pronged plug for an appliance that fits into the three-holed outlet in someone's house. In his 2004 book, *Jacob's Ladder*, he gives the following example of how the chemical plug and outlet work:

> A DNA sequence in a gene for making a protein might look like this: AAAAAAAAAAAAAAAAAAAAAAAAA. Messenger RNA fits to each A with a U (instead of the DNA's T). It carries the copy of the message to the ribosome like this: UUUUUUUUUUUUUUUUUUUUUUUUU. Transfer RNA plugs into the message and reads it like this: UUU UUU UUU UUU UUU UUU UUU UUU. UUU is the chemical code for an **amino acid**, a chemical that is one building block of a protein. The UUU specifies an amino acid called phenylalanine. Now, the cell can construct phenylalanine and build the proteins do the cell's work. A cell can build fifteen amino acids every second with this DNA/RNA system. Because of it, cells know what to do, what proteins to make, and even when to start and stop functions. There are even

codes that specify when the tRNA should "start" and "stop" reading the instructions.[13]

GROWING A BODY

Most genes and DNA for building proteins are the same for everyone. They make humans into humans, mice into mice, and plants into plants. Some genetic instructions, however, are unique to each individual. These genes have been there ever since the person was just a single cell–a fertilized egg called a **zygote**. It is in the formation of the zygote that variation and the uniqueness of each individual are determined.

A zygote is formed from the union of the egg and sperm cells that carry information from both parents. Their DNA combines to create a unique human being. Egg and sperm cells have half the chromosomes of other cells. Each was formed from a parent cell in the mother and father by first splitting into two identical cells each. Then each chromosome is lined up beside its double and exchanges DNA with the other. This mixing and matching is called **recombination** and ensures that the genetic information in each sex cell is unique. Next, the sex cells divide by a process called meiosis and split the chromosome pairs into separate sex cells. Now each sex cell is not only unique but carries only half the normal number of chromosomes. Each sperm or egg cell has only 23 chromosomes, not 46. The 23 pairs of chromosomes are united in the zygote when the egg and sperm fuse their nuclei. The resulting zygote has half its genetic information from the mother and half from the father. It also has the correct number of chromosomes for humans.

The zygote grows by cell division, or mitosis. Its cells multiply, group together to form layers, and then specialize into all the organs of a growing baby. During its first cell divisions, it is called an **embryo**. After eight weeks of growth, it is known as a **fetus** until the baby is born. This newborn individual carries information inherited from both its parents. It is made of trillions of cells. Almost all of them carry the complete genetic code in their nuclei. Even though most of the instructions are turned off in each cell, the pertinent instructions ensure that the cells behave as they were coded to do. While the fetus was developing, they determined what the new individual would look like, whether it would be male or female, what color the eyes would be, and even kinds of diseases to which the person would be vulnerable. Genes determine the traits, characteristics, or conditions with which people are born. Discovering how genes determine traits, however, can be very complicated because many genes often work together. Yet, this is just what scientists have to do if they want to know why different people inherit different diseases or the tendency to develop certain diseases.

GENES AND TRAITS

Genes, just like chromosomes, come in pairs. One gene is inherited from the mother; the other comes from the father. When the genes determine a trait such as eye color, the way they work is easy to understand. If a baby inherits a gene for brown eyes from its mother and a gene for blue eyes from its father, it will have brown eyes. That is because brown is **dominant**, and the gene for blue is **recessive**. Scientists can easily predict the expression of eye color because only one gene determines the trait. The individual will always have the blue-eyed gene, but it will never be expressed. If that person grows up and has a child, however, he or she will still pass on the gene for blue eyes. If the gene is paired with a blue-eyed gene from the other parent in the zygote, then the recessive genes will be expressed. The resulting baby will have blue eyes.

Some diseases work in this simple way, too. Cystic fibrosis, for instance, is a lung and digestive disease that is

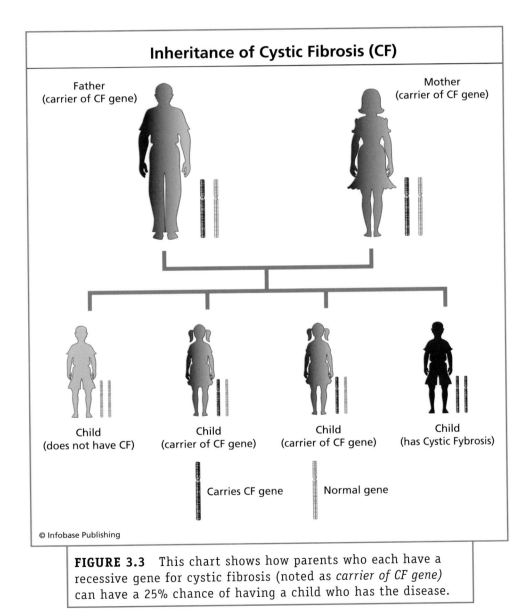

Inheritance of Cystic Fibrosis (CF)

Father
(carrier of CF gene)

Mother
(carrier of CF gene)

Child
(does not have CF)

Child
(carrier of CF gene)

Child
(carrier of CF gene)

Child
(has Cystic Fybrosis)

Carries CF gene

Normal gene

© Infobase Publishing

FIGURE 3.3   This chart shows how parents who each have a recessive gene for cystic fibrosis (noted as *carrier of CF gene)* can have a 25% chance of having a child who has the disease.

inherited, just as eye color is. It is a recessive gene. If two normal parents that carry the recessive gene have a baby, it is possible that the child may inherit that recessive gene from both parents. If so, the child will have cystic fibrosis. If the child inherits only one cystic fibrosis gene, he or she will be healthy but carry the gene throughout life. A few diseases are carried as dominant genes. Huntington's disease is a fatal disease of the brain that appears in adulthood. The gene for this disease is dominant. Anyone who inherits even one gene from one parent will get this disease.

If all tendencies to disease were inherited in this simple way, scientists would have no trouble understanding and predicting disease. Few traits, however, are dependent on just one or two genes. Most genes in the body form linkages with each other; all the genes in the body typically function not independently, but as a giant network. Many groups of genes seem to be inherited together. There is no one gene, for example, that dictates, "This is a human being, not a mouse." Nor is there a single gene that dictates, "This person will get diabetes." Finding genes or groups of genes that dictate certain body functions is extremely difficult.

THE HUMAN GENOME PROJECT

Today, scientists are using a new tool to identify the genes that may be involved in diseases. It is called the Human Genome Project. This is a worldwide effort to completely map the DNA in humans, that is, to list every chemical letter of the bases on the DNA ladder. It is also an effort to identify, name, and locate every gene in each chromosome and to discover the function of every gene. It is a massive undertaking. The entire genome for humans was completely mapped in 2003. This means that scientists now know the structure and sequence of the genome. But this does not mean they can find every gene. Since genes are just sequences of base pairs on the DNA ladder, figuring out exactly where they start and stop is not easy. Genes are strung like pearls up the DNA ladder, but in between them are thousands of bases with no known function. Even within genes, there are stretches of DNA, called **introns**, that do not seem to code for anything. Figuring out the sequence that functions as a gene is difficult. Even figuring out how many genes there are is difficult. So far, the project's scientists estimate that

INTRONS AND GENES

Since introns were first discovered in 1977, scientists have wondered why they are there at all. They have been called "junk" because they do not code for anything, but many scientists believe that they have a purpose. Otherwise, why are there so many introns in human DNA? Scientists initially thought that introns were genes that once had a purpose but are no longer a functioning part of the human genome. However, they now theorize that introns could have many functions. Some introns have been shown to regulate the expression of genes. Others may be markers that help genes shuffle around during recombination and ensure that pieces of genes recombine. This may help new genes to be created and life forms to evolve. Still others might make it possible for one gene to code for several similar proteins; the introns would be signals that indicate which protein code should be read for which function. Introns have been discovered that can signal RNA to remove them and then splice the RNA back together. No one knows for sure, but scientists now believe that much is left to be discovered about the function of introns.

humans have about 30,000 genes, but they have not identified the function of more than 50% of them.

WHEN THE CODE GOES WRONG

The Human Genome Project is a work in progress. Knowing the structure of the genome does not tell scientists what traits are dependent on which genes. Little by little, genetic scientists are identifying genes and learning their roles in healthy human functioning. One way to understand the roles of genes is to discover what happens when a gene is missing or carries a **mutation**. A mutation is a change in a gene, a mistake in the DNA coding. Scientists say DNA is like a giant book, and a mutation is a typographical error. Everyone has such mistakes in the DNA of the genome. Usually, these mistakes do no harm. Since the genes function as a network, they often can compensate for the coding error. Other times, such mutations may actually be helpful. They may help an animal or a species gain traits that help them to survive. Sometimes, however, mutations lead to genetic diseases or disabilities.

Mutations can occur at many points. They can occur when chromosomes are dividing to replicate themselves; they may occur during the recombination process as genes get shuffled around; and they also can be passed along to future generations as inherited traits. When the latter occurs, the DNA instructions inherited by the new individual are faulty. Cell functions and hence body functions may work improperly or not at all. James D. Watson is one of the genetic scientists who discovered the shape and structure of the DNA ladder. In his book, *DNA: The Secret of Life*, he explains how disastrous a typographical error in the "words" of a DNA instruction can be:

A DNA code string can be imagined to look something like this: JIMATETHEFATCAT. The letters form genetic words when they are read by transfer RNA, in groups of 3: JIM ATE THE FAT CAT. The sentence is clear, and the words make sense. A mutation might be something as small as losing the first T (the one in ATE) from the sentence. One base letter is now missing. But transfer RNA still reads the letters in groups of three: JIM AET HEF ATC AT. Nothing makes sense anymore.

DNA letters are limited to ATCG, but the idea is the same as in Watson's example. The direction for making a protein is wrong, and the resulting protein may not function. This is what happens when a genetic mutation occurs, and such DNA mutations are the cause of many inherited diseases.[14]

When just a single DNA mutation causes a disease, it is fairly easy for scientists today to identify the error. When they discover a mutation and see the dysfunction that it causes in the cell, they know what that particular gene is for. They can pinpoint which gene is responsible for the disease. When multiple genes are involved, however, with multiple mutations, it can be very complicated to track down the errors. This is the case with diseases such as diabetes. Multiple genes, not one gene, contribute to developing the disease.

GENES IN THE ENVIRONMENT

Understanding diabetes is even more complex because genes do not operate in isolation. The network of the human genome functions in an environment—at first the environment of the mother's womb and then the environment of the world. Environment includes everything from what a woman eats while she is pregnant to a person's childhood experiences to the kind of exercise the person gets. It includes the germs people are exposed to and the places that they live. Scientists are fairly certain that the cause of diabetes lies in both the environment and genes. Even the Human Genome Project cannot yet determine how much of the cause is the environment and how much is genes. However, an understanding of genes is already helping people with diabetes to lead healthier lives.

4

GENETIC ENGINEERING AND HUMAN INSULIN

Genetic engineering is using science to make changes in genes and their structure. The first genetic engineering success involved insulin, and it began with a quick meeting in a bar on April 7, 1976, in San Francisco. Businessman Bob Swanson asked for the meeting. He wanted to persuade Herb Boyer, a genetic scientist, to form a genetic engineering company. Boyer was not very interested. He was a professor at the University of California in San Francisco and devoted to his laboratory. He was easygoing and not too sure about dealing with a conservative, financial type. Swanson pressed, however, and finally Boyer agreed to a 10-minute meeting in his lab. The two men may have been quite different, but they liked each other immediately. The 10 minutes stretched to hours. They spent that Friday afternoon talking about the possibility of using Boyer's knowledge to start a new kind of business. The result of their fateful meeting was the world's first biotechnology company. The two men named the new company Genentech, which stood for *gen*etic *en*gineering *tech*nology. Its first goal was to develop human insulin using DNA technology.

SLAUGHTERHOUSE PANCREASES

Of course, people with diabetes had been using insulin since it was discovered in 1922, but it was not human insulin. It was purified from the pancreases of cows and pigs. This insulin had saved many lives, but there were problems. The pancreases generally came from slaughterhouses, and for decades there was enough insulin for all people with diabetes. Since the 1920s, however, more and more people were living longer lives with diabetes. This meant that millions of people were dependent on insulin for longer periods of time. By the 1970s, 8 million people in the United States alone used insulin. Some people wondered if the animal supply of insulin could continue to meet the demand.

Insulin from animals sometimes caused difficulties, too. The insulin from animals is very similar to that of people, but not exactly the same. The proteins that make up animal insulin are slightly different from those in human insulin. Some people's bodies reacted badly to this foreign material: Some developed allergies, while others made antibodies to the "foreign invader." This was not deadly, as a rule, but these people developed rashes and welts at their injection sites, and it was very uncomfortable. Also, the antibodies slowed the body's absorption of the insulin. This meant that, over time, more and more insulin had to be injected.

THE GENETIC TEAM

Boyer thought he could produce better insulin for people. He and his partner, Stanley Cohen, were experts in genes and DNA at a time when few people really understood or had an interest in genetic engineering. The two did not know the human genome yet, but they were knowledgeable about genes. They worked, not with people's genes, but with bacteria. They would use bacteria to **clone** human insulin

DNA, making millions of copies of the pieces of DNA to produce insulin for people to use. James D. Watson explains that cloning with genes involves steps much like the word processing function of cutting, pasting, and copying. Boyer was an expert at the cutting part, and Cohen knew how to paste.[15] Bacteria would do the copying for them.

BACTERIA AS A TOOL FOR PRODUCING DNA

A bacterium is a single-celled creature, but it is a complex factory, just like the cells in human bodies. It has a nucleus with genes that carry DNA instructions for the healthy functioning of the organism. Within the cytoplasm of bacteria, however, are structures that human cells do not have. They are **plasmids**, little loops of DNA that are passed on to future generations of bacteria along with the DNA of the

GENENTECH

Genentech is a thriving biotechnology company with three campuses, multiple laboratories, about 700 scientists, and more than 10,000 employees. Genentech works on developing new medicines and genetic engineering techniques. Using recombinant DNA technology, Genentech has produced cancer medicines, asthma treatments, and a human growth hormone, as well as human insulin. A major area of research is the immune system. A whole department at Genentech is devoted to understanding T cells. Scientists are trying to understand the immune system so that they can prevent, reverse, or treat autoimmune disorders like type 1 diabetes. They believe that by learning exactly what is happening inside cells they can someday develop treatments for many diseases.

nucleus. Bacteria reproduce by cell division. In the presence of enough food and a good environment, a bacterium grows slightly larger. Its DNA replicates, or copies itself, and then the cell divides, splitting into two daughter cells. Each is an identical copy of the parent cell, with a nucleus containing the complete genome. Each plasmid also is replicated in the daughter cells. The daughter cells of many bacteria can replicate themselves in as little as 20 minutes. This means a bacterial colony can double in size every 20 minutes. Theoretically, one bacterium could become one billion within 10 hours. This never happens outside the laboratory because bacteria in natural environments do not have enough food, but Boyer and Cohen knew that if they could change the DNA in the plasmids of just one bacterium, they could have a colony numbering in the millions in their lab.

Plasmids to Cut and Paste

The scientists already knew how to alter the DNA of a plasmid. First, the plasmid had to be cut so that a new DNA sequence could be fitted into it. **Restriction enzymes** could do the cutting. Restriction enzymes are proteins in bacteria that help to protect them from infections. They can be thought of as part of a bacterium's immune system. Viruses often infect and kill bacteria, so bacteria need a defense. Viruses are just packages of DNA. Restriction enzymes recognize foreign DNA sequences and are the scissors that seek out and cut the attacking DNA. Each bacterial restriction enzyme cuts a specific viral DNA sequence. For example, the enzyme named *Eco*R1 cuts the DNA string GAATTC. This viral DNA is destroyed whenever it is cut, and the bacterium stays healthy. Boyer was one of the discoverers of *Eco*R1. He knew how to isolate and use restriction enzymes in the lab to cut DNA strings. He knew how to cut a plasmid with restriction enzymes so that a new DNA sequence could be added to it.

Cohen was a plasmid expert who knew how to remove a plasmid from a cell. He also knew how to paste the plasmid back together once a new protein instruction had been added to it. He used an enzyme called ligase that glues the ends of DNA together so that the instruction will work correctly. With their combined expertise, the scientists could cut, paste, and then let their bacteria copy an altered plasmid. If they could introduce the DNA instruction for making insulin into the plasmid, they would have an insulin-making bacterial factory. No one was sure it could be done, but Swanson trusted in them, and Genentech devoted all its resources to making it happen. The manipulating of genes and DNA is called **recombinant DNA** technology. It is not the same recombining that chromosomes do in the sex cells. It is the mixing and matching, or the recombining, of two pieces of DNA to form a new, artificial DNA sequence.

Insulin from Bacteria

The scientists of Genentech already knew the gene in humans that coded for insulin production. Even though the entire human genome was not yet mapped, the insulin gene had been discovered. They decided to add this human gene to the plasmid in a harmless kind of bacterium called *Escherichia coli*. This strain of *E. coli* bacterium is not the kind that causes disease. It is a harmless strain of *E. coli* that lives naturally in people's digestive systems. The trouble was that the human insulin gene was full of introns, as are all human genes. Bacteria have no introns (just as humans have no plasmids) and so are unable to read around them when manufacturing proteins. To solve this problem, Genentech scientists had to make copies of the parts of the gene that actually coded for insulin using

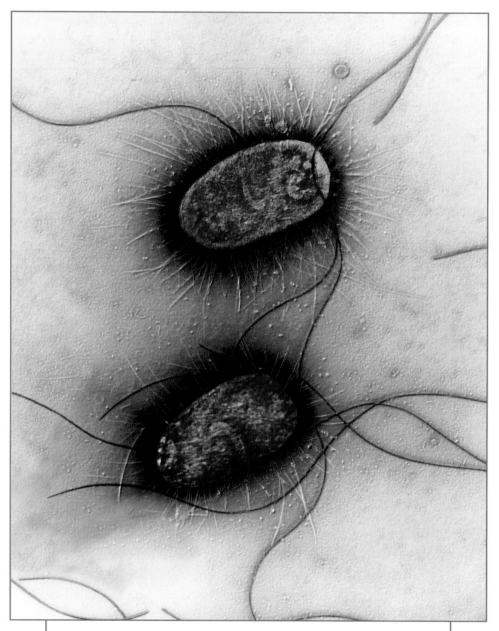

FIGURE 4.1   A weakened strain of the bacterium *Escherichia coli*, a common inhabitant of the human digestive tract, is used in recombinant DNA technology.

chemicals in their lab. Then they had DNA sequences that a bacterium's RNA could read.

Next, they cut the plasmids with restriction enzymes and inserted the human DNA sequence. The plasmids were

FRANKENSTEIN'S BACTERIA?

Recombinant DNA was a suspect and frightening technology when it was first introduced. The public, many politicians, and some scientists worried that "playing God" with bacterial genes could result in a monstrous disease. Throughout the world, governments stepped in and placed restrictions and regulations on any laboratory that was recombining human DNA. These restrictions did not affect Genentech because researchers there were making copies of DNA rather than using DNA itself. It was a loophole that made it easier for them to develop human insulin. Biogen, an English biotechnology company founded around the same time as Genentech, also was trying to make human insulin. Its scientists, however, were using human DNA. They had to function under containment regulations that ensured no killer virus or bacterium could escape into society. They were required to work in a biological warfare laboratory where they could be sealed off from the world. Researchers had to wear special clothing, sterilize everything that went into and out of the lab, and shower before they left each day. These restrictions slowed them down so much that they lost the race to clone human insulin to Genentech. Today, this simple recombinant DNA technology is considered so safe that college students can experiment with the techniques. It is routinely used to make human insulin, but in the 1970s, many people were wary of recombinant DNA.

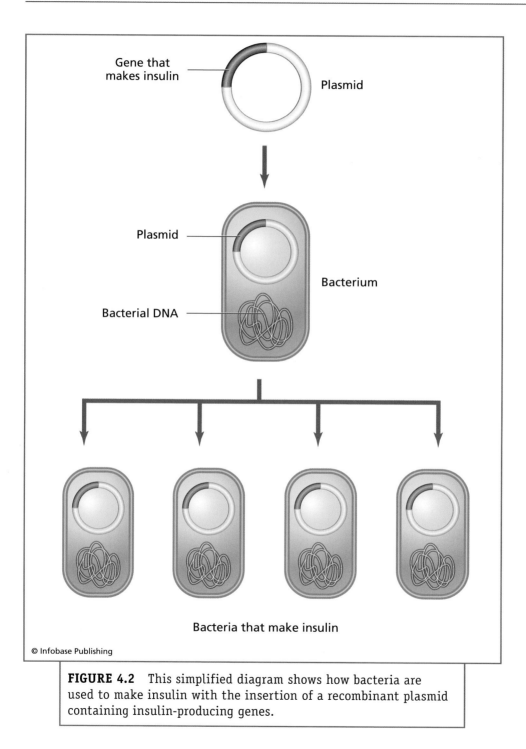

Gene that
makes insulin

Plasmid

Plasmid

Bacterium

Bacterial DNA

Bacteria that make insulin

© Infobase Publishing

FIGURE 4.2 This simplified diagram shows how bacteria are used to make insulin with the insertion of a recombinant plasmid containing insulin-producing genes.

glued back together with ligase. The insulin gene was now recombined with the bacteria's plasmids. The cut and pasted plasmids carried the DNA sequence that coded for making human insulin. They were reinserted into the bacteria, and the bacteria were allowed to divide and multiply into a whole colony. Each bacterium carried the plasmid information for making human insulin. The DNA sequence successfully instructed each bacterial cell to make human insulin. The scientists did this with many bacteria and ended up with huge colonies of genetically engineered bacteria. Bacteria are very good at the copying part of the process. Soon, the scientists were ready to harvest their crop—insulin—and purify it. They had engineered synthetic human insulin. This human insulin was first sold to people with diabetes in 1982.

Human Insulin Today

Producing human insulin was the first biotechnology and genetic engineering success. Genentech began the whole biotechnology industry with its synthetic human insulin from bacteria. It developed a safe medical treatment that benefited millions of people. It meant that there was no chance of an insulin shortage endangering people with diabetes. Human insulin is much less likely than animal insulin to cause people's bodies to develop antibodies or an allergic reaction. The insulin is also absorbed by the body more quickly and therefore works faster.

Today, the process of making recombinant human insulin has been dramatically improved. It is faster and cheaper than it was when Boyer and Cohen first developed the technology. Scientists still make insulin with either bacteria or other simple organisms (yeasts). The insulin they produce is as pure and perfect as the insulin produced in the human body by the pancreas. Scientists no longer have to chemically copy the insulin gene to get rid of the introns. Instead, they use a process that uses human messenger RNA. It has already edited out the introns when it read the DNA in the human insulin gene. Scientists can reverse the message and make a copy of DNA from the messenger RNA

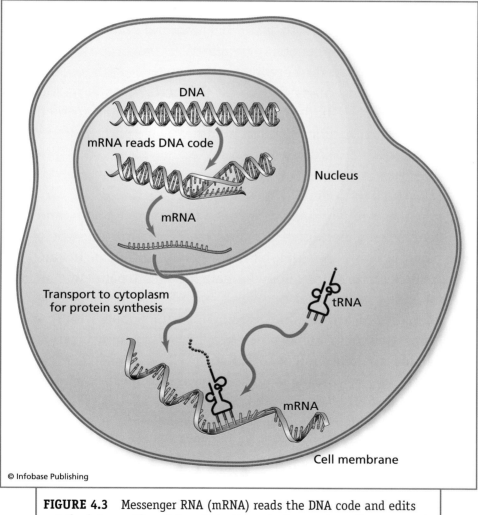

© Infobase Publishing

FIGURE 4.3 Messenger RNA (mRNA) reads the DNA code and edits out the introns. Then it travels to the cytoplasm, where the corrected message is read in groups of three by the transfer RNA (tRNA).

that carries only the coding for insulin and is cleaned of introns. This DNA sequence is pasted into the bacteria or yeasts, which then produce the proteins for insulin.

Almost all the insulin in use in the United States is synthetic insulin. It is usually called Humulin™, which is the name given to it by Eli Lilly, the company that supported Genentech financially when Boyer, Cohen, and Swanson were first struggling to produce human insulin. (It was also the company that produced and sold the animal insulin used for decades before biotechnology became a reality.) Humulin™ comes in several different forms now, too. One form, called Humalog™, is referred to as the mealtime insulin. It goes to work within minutes of injection so that a person with diabetes can inject and then eat right away. It acts almost as fast as insulin produced by the pancreas. Slow-acting Humulin™ is released steadily into the body over several hours. It takes longer to reach the bloodstream and is powerful for a longer time than the fast-acting Humalog™. With a combination of the two, a person with diabetes can test blood sugars and then make a decision to inject whichever insulin is needed. This helps prevent hypoglycemic episodes (which could result from fast-acting insulin) and also allows a sudden decision to eat a meal, which could cause hyperglycemia without an extra dose of insulin.

Genetic engineering for human insulin is a true success story and has improved the treatment of diabetes around the world. It is still just a treatment, however, and it did not lead to an understanding of what causes diabetes. Even the identification of the gene that codes for insulin production does not explain why people get diabetes. The next goal of genetic scientists is to identify the genes related to diabetes and to find the mutations or variations in the genes that actually contribute to or cause diabetes.

GENES AND
TYPE 1 DIABETES

Scientists know that multiple genetic variations must be involved in the onset of type 1 diabetes. Since type 1 is an autoimmune disease, they strongly suspect that some or most of these are immune system genes. Searching for the genetic cause of type 1 diabetes involves both identifying genes gone awry in the immune system and looking for any other genes that may be involved. Scientists do not know why most people's pancreases are not harmed by common viral illnesses, while other people end up with destroyed beta cells. It is not enough to know that type 1 diabetes is an autoimmune disease. A virus may start the autoimmune destruction, but other environmental factors could be operating, too. Looking for the true cause of type 1 diabetes is not simple, but scientists, like detectives, are searching for clues and slowly identifying the different factors that lead to diabetes.

VALUABLE IDENTICAL TWINS

The first question for the scientific detectives was determining how large a role genes play in the onset of type 1 diabetes. This is often done with studies of identical twins.

Identical twins share the same genes. That means that their DNA is almost identical. If type 1 diabetes were caused exclusively by genetic information, then one twin could never have diabetes unless the other had it, too. If type 1 were caused partly by genes and partly by the environment, then it would be possible for one twin to have type 1, while the other remained healthy. Twin studies are a good way to estimate how much genes contribute to the development of type 1 diabetes.

In 1988, a team of scientists at Kings College Hospital in London reported on a study of 49 pairs of identical twins. In each case, one twin had been recently diagnosed with type 1 diabetes, while the other did not have the disease. For years, the scientists followed the twins. They discovered that even after 24 years, only 34% of the healthy twins developed diabetes. These results have been confirmed by many other scientific studies. Some studies found diabetes developing in both twins more often, perhaps 50% of the time. But no study found that both twins in a pair got type 1 diabetes 100% of the time. When one twin has the disease, the chance of the other developing diabetes is only 30% to 50%.

In other studies, scientists found that family history can increase the chance of getting type 1 diabetes, but not by very much. If a parent or sibling (a nonidentical brother or sister) has type 1, it increases the risk to about 5% to 6%. (For perspective, the risk of getting type 1 diabetes when no one in a family has the disease is about 0.4%.) This means that genes play a role in the development of type 1 but are not the sole cause of the disease. Genes are no more than half the cause of type 1 diabetes. The environment must be responsible for the other half of the problem.

WHERE DO YOU LIVE?

Scientists have also compared the incidences of type 1 diabetes for different races. They have discovered that type 1 diabetes is most common in Caucasians and rare in African Americans and Asians. This could be due to different genes being more common in different populations, but type 1 diabetes varies by country, too. Finland, for example, has the highest number of type 1 diabetics in the world. Estonia, a nearby country with a very genetically similar population, has only one-third the number of type 1 diabetics. Even scientists find these facts confusing. There must be a genetic component to type 1 diabetes, yet there have to be environmental causes that vary from country to country. One

FINLAND'S DILEMMA

Since the 1950s, the number of young people with type 1 diabetes has quadrupled in Finland. Finnish scientists are trying to understand why this has happened and to figure out a way to slow the epidemic. One study of Finland's at-risk children is called DIPP (Diabetes Prediction and Prevention Project). It began in 1994 and has continued to the present. Researchers have found more than 8,500 children with HLA genes that predict an increased risk for developing diabetes. They test these children for autoantibodies, and if they are present, the scientists include the children in a study of insulin that can be given through the nose in a nasal spray. Some children get the insulin and others get a spray with no active ingredient (this is called a placebo) so that scientists can determine if the insulin has any protective effect. This kind of experiment scientist suggests that diabetes genes are like a loaded gun. Something in the environment has to pull the trigger before type 1 can develop. Around the world, different scientific teams search for both environmental and genetic factors that may increase the chances of getting type 1 diabetes.

IMMUNE SYSTEM GENES

So far, genetic scientists have found about 18 regions on the human genome that seem to increase the risk for developing type 1 diabetes. These regions have multiple genes, most of which have not yet been identified.

Each human chromosome is one long strand of DNA. The chromosome pairs have been numbered by genetic

is called a double-blind study. Neither the subjects nor the researcher knows who is getting the insulin and who is getting the placebo. When the study is over, Finnish scientists hope to know if giving insulin before type 1 develops can prevent it from occurring. This idea is based on some animal studies that suggest that extra insulin can calm the immune system and slow or prevent attacks in the future.

Other Finnish studies have examined flu epidemics and early childhood diet to see if they increase the risk for type 1 diabetes. One study examined the effect of flu vaccines on the risk for type 1, but it found no difference among children who were vaccinated and those who were not. Unraveling the cause of Finland's growing population of diabetes in its youth is proving very difficult.

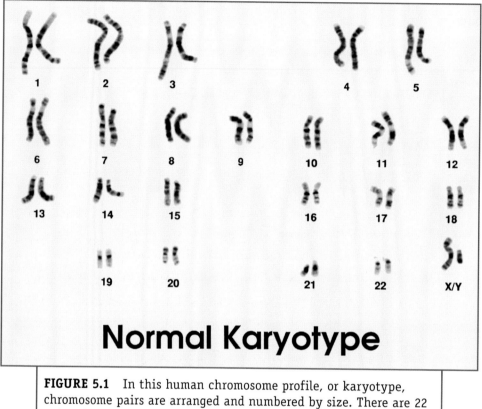

Normal Karyotype

FIGURE 5.1 In this human chromosome profile, or karyotype, chromosome pairs are arranged and numbered by size. There are 22 pairs of numbered chromosomes and one pair of sex-determining chromosomes. These are the chromosomes of a male. How do we know? There is one X chromosome and one Y chromosome.

scientists according to their size, from 1 to 22 (the X and Y chromosomes for determining sex are not assigned a number). Located on chromosome 6 are human leukocyte antigen (HLA) genes. They are of critical interest to diabetes researchers. HLA genes help T cells to find and recognize foreign invaders. The T cells check the cells to see if they are self or nonself. If the cells are a virus or bacterium, T cells set off attacks against them. They direct other immune system cells to make antibodies against the invaders. Without HLA genes, these attacks would not be possible, because T cells would not be able to find the germs.

Usually, this system of HLA genes aiding T cells works very well. HLA genes, however, come in several variations, just as genes for eye color do. Some variations seem to help T cells to avoid making mistakes, such as attacking cells that are self. Others do not seem to have any effect on T cells' ability to recognize foreign proteins. Some variations of HLA genes raise the risk of an autoimmune attack and type 1 diabetes.

DR AND DQ GENES

One kind of HLA variation, named DR2 by scientists, appears to protect people from diabetes. Few people with this gene variation ever develop diabetes. Two variations, however, are known to increase the risk of developing type 1 diabetes. They have been labeled DR3 and DR4. These variations seem to make it difficult for T cells to distinguish between self and nonself. Genetic scientists have studied the HLA regions of people with and without type 1 diabetes. They discovered that only about half of all people have either DR3 or DR4 genes in their genetic makeup. Only 3% of the population has both genes. However, 95% of Caucasian people with type 1 diabetes have at least one of the genes. DR3 and DR4 account for 40% to 50% of the genetic risk of developing type 1 diabetes.

Exactly how DR3 and DR4 genes lead to diabetes is unclear to scientists. Some people with these genes get type 1 diabetes, but others do not. To make things even more complicated, DR genes do not operate in the simple dominant/recessive pattern of eye color or cystic fibrosis. Instead, the genes have varying degrees of what is termed **penetrance**. This means they are neither completely

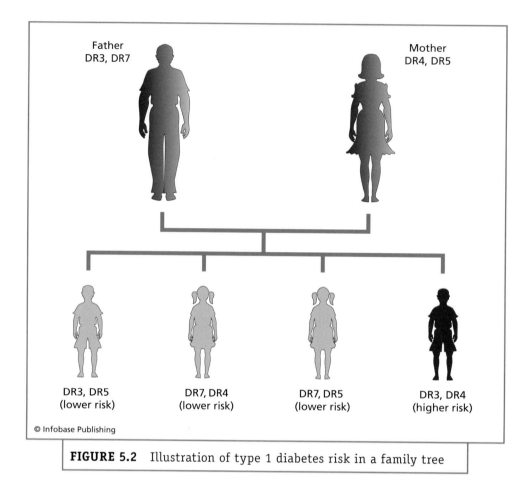

FIGURE 5.2 Illustration of type 1 diabetes risk in a family tree

dominant nor completely recessive. Some of the trait coded for by the gene will be expressed, especially if it is linked with other genes, even when only one variant is present in a person's genome. Yet this does not happen all the time, as it would with a dominant gene. Other gene linkages can suppress the trait somewhat. This variability in penetrance is called incomplete penetrance by genetic scientists.

DR genes are usually inherited together with other genes, called DQ genes. They are part of the HLA group, too. Some DQ genes protect against diabetes, but others seem to increase the risk, since they show up more often in people with type 1 diabetes than in healthy people. So far, it is very difficult for scientists to tell which kind of genes are more important—the DR genes or the DQ genes. The variations that increase risk are too often linked and inherited together. All scientists can say is that inheriting these gene variations increases susceptibility to type 1 diabetes.

ANTIBODIES AGAINST BETA CELLS

One symptom that is linked with HLA genes is the development of **autoantibodies**. These are antibodies made by the immune system against the beta cells of the pancreas. They indicate that the immune system has mistakenly recognized beta cells as foreign invaders and attacked them. The antibodies are ready and waiting to attack any other beta cells that might "invade" in the future. Scientists can identify these antibodies in people's blood. Interestingly, these antibodies can be found in people who have not developed type 1 diabetes. They have been found in family members of people with type 1 diabetes, and they have been found in people who later developed type 1 diabetes. (Beta cells can be attacked and destroyed without causing diabetes. Type 1 diabetes does not develop until 80% of the beta cells have been destroyed.)

In 2006, P.J. Bingley and E.A. Gale at the University of Bristol in England did a study of people who had autoantibodies to beta cells. There were 549 people in the study, from 20 different countries, and all of them had a parent or sibling with type 1 diabetes. The people were of all different ages, both children and adults. The scientific team followed them all for five years, waiting to see which ones would develop diabetes. Only 11% of the adults older than 25 eventually developed type 1 diabetes, even though they had autoantibodies for beta cells. However, 62% of people younger than 25 developed type 1 diabetes within five years.[16] The presence of autoantibodies to beta cells greatly increases the risk of type 1 in young people, but it still does not predict with certainty who will get diabetes and who will not.

ON CHROMOSOME 11

Other scientists who have studied other genes associated with diabetes found similar results. They could identify genes and variations that increased the risk of diabetes, but they could never find a gene or group of genes that always cause type 1 diabetes. Scientists estimate that at least 10 genes must have mutations before a susceptibility to type 1 diabetes will develop. One area they have studied is on chromosome 11, which is the location of the insulin gene. Close to the insulin gene is a string of DNA. The order of the bases at this site varies among people. Scientists have discovered that certain orders can increase the risk of getting type 1 by a factor of three. No one knows, however, exactly how the presence of variations in this area increases risk. Some scientists believe that the area may signal T cells or other white blood cells in the immune system.

NOD MICE AND THE MIF GENE

One of the most important ways that researchers hunt for diabetes genes is with laboratory mice. The mice they work with are called knockout mice because one or more of their genes has been deactivated or changed. If that gene plays a role in the development of diabetes, the mice will develop type 1 diabetes. Then, scientists can discover exactly which gene is involved and experiment both with how to cause the problem and how to prevent it. Knockout mice with type 1 diabetes are called NOD (non-obese diabetic) mice, and there are many different strains. Mice make ideal research subjects because 95% of their genes are identical to human genes. The role played by HLA genes was first discovered with NOD mice.

In 2005, researcher Yousef Al-Abed used NOD mice to discover an important gene involved in type 1 diabetes in an unusual way. He had two kinds of NOD mice. One strain carried a gene called the MIF gene. The other strain was missing this gene. The MIF gene makes a protein that is an immune system messenger, and apparently it is a message that tells the immune system to attack beta cells. Mice without this gene did not develop type 1 diabetes, even when Al-Abed gave them a chemical that causes diabetes. Mice with functioning MIF genes got type 1 diabetes 100% of the time. Al-Abed says, "The MIF gene may be regulating other genes involved in type 1 diabetes. We don't know yet, but we're looking into this."[17]

A **regulator gene** is one that turns on or off the expression of other genes. If MIF is a regulator gene, it may be critical to the development of diabetes. It may partially control how HLA genes work, as well as what happens near the insulin gene on chromosome 11. Another regulator gene was discovered by Dr. Jin-Xiong She in 2004. It has been named SUMO-4. Dr. She found that when a mutation of SUMO-4 encounters an environmental trigger, such as a bacterial or viral infection, it begins an autoimmune response that eventually attacks the patient's own cells.

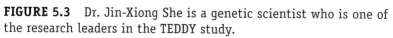

FIGURE 5.3 Dr. Jin-Xiong She is a genetic scientist who is one of the research leaders in the TEDDY study.

GENES AND ENVIRONMENT TOGETHER

Scientists are making good progress in finding the genes that contribute to type 1 diabetes, but they still have a long way to go. Even when they have identified all the genes that can lead to type 1 diabetes, they will still have only about half the answer. To find the trigger that sets off the disease, they must look to the environment. This is the goal of TEDDY, which stands for The Environmental Determinants of Diabetes in the Young. It is a massive long-term study of newborn children in four U.S. states and in Finland, Sweden, and Germany. The study began in October 2005. Dr. She is one of the leaders. He and the large TEDDY team will screen the genes of 220,800 babies, searching for those with the genes that seem to increase the risk for type 1 diabetes. They believe that about 13,000 babies will carry the genes that make them susceptible to type 1 diabetes, and about half of those children will eventually develop the disease. The scientists will follow these babies for at least 15 years and try to find the environmental triggers that led to diabetes.

There are two main environmental suspects. The first is a viral illness. The babies' families will record every illness, every time they give the babies medicine, and every doctor's visit. Researchers will visit the families every three months to collect the data. Another major environmental suspect is cow's milk. Scientists have discovered that breastfeeding seems to protect infants from future diabetes. The team will record whatever the babies eat, from cow's milk to first drinks of water to the first cookies. Someday, they will have a massive amount of information to compare as they search for the environmental factors that the children have in common. Since some scientists believe that the environment of the mother's uterus may be what triggers type 1 diabetes, the researchers will also interview each mother about her pregnancy. They will ask for all the details of her pregnancy, including what she ate and if she ever got sick.

The goal of TEDDY is to try to find changes in the immune system that occur in the first years of life. If the scientists can link these changes both to genes and to environmental factors, they may actually discover the true causes of type 1 diabetes. But as one TEDDY scientist says, "The bottom line is that it's not going to be a simple answer."[18]

GENES AND
TYPE 2 DIABETES

Mary Thomas has struggled with type 2 diabetes since she was 17 years old. Today, she is more than 60 years of age and must use insulin and oral medications to keep her illness under control. She fights to lose weight but finds it almost impossible. She works hard to avoid the terrible complications that type 2 can cause. Her mother had diabetes and died of heart disease at age 68. Many of her neighbors and friends have suffered complications such as kidney disease, amputations, and strokes. So far, Thomas has been able to avoid all these problems, and she knows she is lucky. She worries, however, about her people and about others with diabetes. Thomas is a Native American of the Pima tribe, but she notices that all people in the United States are getting bigger and heavier. She knows diet is much to blame. She says that the Pima used to eat a lean diet of fish, game, beans, and whole grains, but with the arrival of white people, "There was an onslaught of salts and sweets."[19] This altered diet, combined with the genes with which people are born, has led to an explosion of type 2 diabetes among the Pima and all Native Americans.

One Pima Indian woman with diabetes says, "What I really want to do is change the way we eat here." She has a mother who died from kidney complications of diabetes. Her father had to have a foot amputated because of diabetes. Four of her brothers and sisters have diabetes. She is a mother of three girls, and she is determined to keep them from the fate of her family. She tries hard to protect them with healthy foods and regular exercise.[20] Scientists know that environment, especially diet and exercise, can be a major factor in the development of type 2 diabetes. Genetic factors, however, may determine the outcome for the three girls, despite their mother's best efforts. They may be able to delay the onset of diabetes, but they may not be able to prevent it altogether.

WHO IS AT RISK?

Like type 1 diabetes, type 2 diabetes is difficult to understand on the genetic level. It appears to be caused by multiple genes and environmental triggers. It may even be several different diseases with different causes, all leading to high blood glucose levels. Scientists have to explore genes, environment, and families to understand how type 2 diabetes develops. Scientists know that type 2 diabetes usually develops in overweight people, that most people are adults when it develops, and that it runs in families. Studies of identical twins yielded surprising results. Type 2 diabetes has a much stronger genetic component than type 1 diabetes. If one twin develops type 2, at least 90% of the time the other twin also will also develop diabetes. If a nonidentical sibling has type 2 diabetes, the risk of developing the disease is 40%. Having two parents with type 2 diabetes increases the risk to about 80%.

Some races and ethnic groups have a greater incidence of type 2 than others, although the disease is common among all peoples. In the United States, African Americans, Mexican Americans, and Native Americans are much more likely to develop type 2 diabetes than Caucasians. Furthermore, the incidence of type 2 is increasing among all ethnic groups and even among all ages. Many scientists consider type 2 diabetes to be an epidemic throughout much of the world. Genes for type 2 diabetes are inherited in families and in ethnic populations, but these genes have been very hard to determine. Since overweight, or obesity, is so highly associated with type 2 diabetes, obesity seems to be a major cause of the disease. Yet most obese people do not get type 2 diabetes; therefore, scientists look for genes that determine obesity but also for genes involved in insulin resistance and insulin production. As with type 1 diabetes, multiple genetic triggers must be involved. Genes for overweight probably interact with other genetic causes. Thanks to the help of Pima Indians, several genetic factors have been identified.

STUDY OF THE PIMA INDIANS

A tribe of about 11,000 Pima Indians lives on the Gila River in Arizona. They have the highest incidence of type 2 diabetes of any group of people in the world. Of all adult Pimas, 50% have type 2 diabetes. More than 95% of these people are overweight. Since 1965, the Pimas have been helping the National Institutes of Health (NIH) and the National Institute of Diabetes and Digestive and Kidney Diseases (NIDDK) to study diabetes. NIH calls the Pimas "pathfinders" who are leading the way in the genetic maze of type 2 diabetes. The Pimas cooperate in genetic studies among their families, and 90% of them have given DNA samples to scientists. With all the data scientists have gathered, they have learned a great deal about type 2 diabetes.

Studies of the Pima Indians led to the proof that diabetes runs in families and that there is a link between type 2 diabetes and obesity. It is also because of the Pimas that scientists learned that insulin resistance occurs before type 2 develops. In each Pima family, researchers look for one parent with type 2 and one who is healthy. Then, they can search the genetic makeup of all the children, looking for the differences in DNA between those who develop diabetes and those who do not. When they find a DNA sequence shared by those with type 2 diabetes, they have a genetic marker. This marker may not be a whole gene; it may be just part of a gene. The marker, however, is a signpost that tells scientists where to search for a gene for type 2 diabetes.

FIGURE 6.1 Three generations of a Zuni family live on the Zuni reservation in western New Mexico.

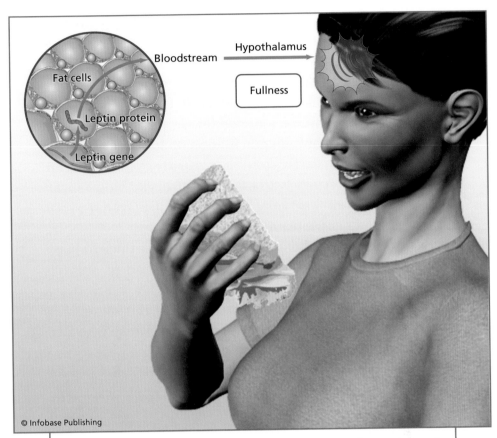

FIGURE 6.2 Leptin in the bloodstream may control appetite and prevent people from overeating and becoming obese.

THRIFTY GENES

One of the first things that scientists discovered is that people with type 2 diabetes have a slower **metabolic rate** than family members who do not get diabetes. This means that food is turned into energy more slowly, energy is used up by the body more slowly, and the individual needs fewer calories to maintain the body than non-diabetics need. Becoming overweight is a common result. Why would some people have a slow metabolic rate? Since 1984, Eric Ravussin, an NIDDK scientist, has been trying to answer that question. Although he has not yet found the gene or genes responsible, he believes that the answer is a "thrifty gene." The idea of a thrifty gene was first proposed in 1962 by geneticist James V. Neel, who hypothesized that those individuals with the thrifty gene were very efficient at taking in and using food. For most of humanity's time on earth, conditions mostly cycled between feast and famine. A gene variant that conserved blood sugar and slowed metabolism may have been a lifesaver. It probably protected people from starvation.

For hundreds of generations, people like the Pima Indians were farmers and hunter-gatherers. They had to survive under difficult conditions. Some seasons or years, they were very successful in getting enough food, but sometimes crops failed and animals were hard to find. Those who survived this feast or famine cycle were the ones able to use food most efficiently. Their cells naturally became insulin resistant in order to cope with the diet. People with slow metabolic rates were able to continue functioning through the lean times. Their thrifty genes let them easily store fat during times of plenty so that they could live off this fat when no food was available. Since they were successful at surviving, they were more likely to have children than people who starved to death. They passed the thrifty gene on to their children.

Until the end of World War II, Pima Indians lived a traditional tribal lifestyle. Their diets contained only about 15% fat. They ate mostly lean proteins, grains, and vegetables. Even though they no longer lived a feast or famine lifestyle, the thrifty gene did them no harm. After World War II, however, Pima Indians on the Gila River began to eat a more American diet. There was always plenty to eat, and much of the food was high in calories and fats. Today, Pima

Indians eat a diet of about 40% fat, just as most Americans do. According to the theory, the thrifty gene makes their bodies work hard to store all this fat in case the famine is coming. But the famine never comes, and Pima Indians—or any people with the thrifty gene—become more and more overweight and insulin-resistant. Ravussin believes this, in part, causes diabetes to develop in Pima Indians. To test his theory, he visited another tribe of Pima Indians who live in Mexico. Their genetic background is very similar to the Pimas of the Gila River. He examined 35 Mexican Pimas who did not eat a high-fat American diet. He found just three cases of diabetes. Most of the tribe's members were not overweight. This was evidence for Ravussin's theory that the thrifty gene leads to obesity and diabetes only when people eat the wrong kinds of foods.

THRIFTY GENES IN OTHER GROUPS

Many scientists believe that thrifty genes explain the epidemic of type 2 diabetes in Native American and African-American populations, among others. The prevalence of type 2 diabetes in some native peoples in Polynesia and Australia is so high that scientists fear they will be wiped out. Biologist Jared Diamond believes that type 2 diabetes is a disease of people rich enough to always have plenty of food. He says that famines in Europe several hundred years ago meant Caucasians had thrifty genes, too. After the famines were over, there was a diabetes epidemic. Those who could afford it ate plentifully, became obese and insulin resistant, and developed diabetes. He thinks this may have wiped out many of the people who had thrifty genes before they ever had children. Those who survived the diabetes epidemic did not have the thrifty gene and did not pass it on to their children. The rural poor of Europe, who never were able to eat a high-fat diet, may have had the thrifty gene, but they did not become obese and did not die of diabetes. Diamond says that their descendants still carry the thrifty gene and are now eating a high-fat diet. Although not as bad as the diabetes epidemic in Pima Indians, there is also an epidemic of diabetes in people of European descent.

Suspect Genes

Obesity does seem to have a genetic cause. No one is sure if part of this cause is the thrifty gene, but scientists have found genetic markers that seem to increase the risk of obesity. One gene that varies among Pima Indians is called FABP2. In people with type 2 diabetes, a variation in this gene seems to make the body absorb more fat from meals. Researchers think that this could also lead to more fat in the blood, and they believe that this fat could cause insulin

VICTIM OF PLENTY

Johann Sebastian Bach was a famous classical composer who lived from 1685 to 1750. He also may have carried the thrifty gene. He lived in Germany during a time when the last of the famines of Europe had ended. Bach was well-to-do, lived comfortably, and was well fed. By age 60, he developed medical problems that suggest to scientists today that he had type 2 diabetes. He probably had high blood pressure. One portrait of him shows his mouth a bit twisted and one eyelid drooping, and this suggests he may have had a mild stroke, which is often the result of untreated high blood pressure. The portrait also shows that he was obese. In later years, he began to go blind and complained of pain in his eyes. One scientist who studied his handwriting noticed that it resistance. Scientists do know that fat in the cells makes cells more resistant to insulin.

In 2007, scientist Edwin Weiss discovered that half of the U.S. population has this variation of FABP2. Weiss gave people rich milkshakes to drink. He discovered that those with the gene variation metabolized the fats differently than the other people without the variant. He says that the gene variation cannot cause diabetes by itself, but it contributes to the risk of type 2 diabetes.

In Pima Indians, NIDDK scientist Leslie Baier has found other DNA variations in people with type 2. A tiny change in a DNA sequence seems to change how the nearby gene called calpain-10 works. This gene is on chromosome 2. People with this change had a lower metabolism and more insulin resistance than people who were not at risk for diabetes. They seemed to store more of the glucose from food

was clearer some times than others. This suggests a possibility of bouts of hypoglycemia, which can make people weak and shaky. All these suggest complications from type 2 diabetes.

If Bach carried the thrifty gene, he could have become overweight because of it and developed insulin resistance and then diabetes. Since his diabetes could not be diagnosed or treated, he would have developed many complications from years of fluctuating sugar levels. Bach actually died of a massive stroke, but did uncontrolled diabetes cause it? An epidemic of diabetes swept throughout Europe during Bach's lifetime, and although no one knows for sure, scientists think he was one of its victims.

they ate rather than burning it for energy. Some scientists say this is just what a thrifty gene would do and wonder if calpain-10 is, in fact, the thrifty gene.

Baier has found areas on several other chromosomes that seem to contribute to both obesity and type 2 diabetes. All of the genetic variations seem to increase the risk for both obesity and insulin resistance. Exactly how this happens, however, is still not well understood. None of the variations found in Pima Indians are unique to them. The variations occur in all groups of people, and probably are responsible for obesity and insulin resistance for any people who develop type 2 diabetes.

LEPTIN RECEPTOR

Leptin is a hormone produced by fat cells in the body. The hormone acts on the brain to control appetite and burn fat stored in the tissues. The degree to which people feel hungry or burn stored fat is partly controlled by the amount of leptin in the blood. This amount is in turn controlled by the leptin receptor (LEPR) gene on chromosome 1. Variations in this gene do not cause diabetes, but some scientists say they increase the risk of obesity. Others do not agree. However, there is evidence that high amounts of leptin are in the blood of obese people, yet their brains do not pick up the signal that they are "full." These people eat more, becoming more obese and increasing the risk of insulin resistance and type 2 diabetes.

GENES FOR NORMAL INSULIN PRODUCTION

The LEPR gene is not the only one that increases obesity risk, and obesity is only one risk factor for diabetes. Finding the genes responsible for type 2 diabetes is incredibly difficult because so many are apparently involved. Scientists have found genetic variations that occur with insulin resistance and type 2 diabetes on many chromosomes, but the interaction is so complicated that they are far from identifying the actual genetic causes of type 2 diabetes. So far, they have found about 20 different areas of the genetic map that seem to increase the risk of insulin resistance and type 2 diabetes. They continue to search for genetic variations and to try to understand what they do in the body, but it is slow going.

One gene variant discovery was reported in 2006. It was found by a large study group, the Diabetes Prevention Program. The gene, named TCF7L2, apparently is involved in producing insulin. People with a common variant of this gene had decreased insulin secretion, which is associated with an increased incidence of diabetes. From

DANGER FOR MANY PEOPLES

Native, or indigenous, people throughout the world face a devastating epidemic of type 2 diabetes when they eat a Western diet. Scientist Paul Zimmet calls the problem the "coca-colonization" of cultures. In Australia, where Zimmet lives, about 20% of the indigenous people have diabetes. In Nauru, a Pacific Island community, almost 50% of the people have diabetes. In Canada, 30% of the native peoples have diabetes. On Australia's Torres Strait Island, 30% of the people have diabetes. Even in China, as it opens up to Western culture, the rate of type 2 diabetes is skyrocketing. The rate of type 2 diabetes for indigenous peoples is disastrous and may mean the extinction of some cultures within 100 years if something does not change. Zimmet says it is the biggest epidemic the world has ever seen.

this study, scientists learned that decreased insulin production as well as insulin resistance could lead to type 2 diabetes.

A scientific team in Australia, working for a company called ChemGenex Pharmaceuticals, made an important diabetes discovery in 2006. It is called the PSARL gene. Scientists do not yet know exactly how the PSARL gene works, but it seems to control the functioning of the cell's **mitochondria**. Mitochondria are organelles found outside the nucleus that are often called the cells' powerhouses. They produce energy for the cells. A variation in the PSARL gene leads to mitochondria that fail to work correctly. This variation is strongly linked to type 2 diabetes. Scientists at ChemGenex did experiments with desert rats to see how the PSARL gene mutation interacts with environmental factors. They discovered that rats with the PSARL gene that roamed around the desert were thin and healthy. Those in cages given lots of food developed obesity and diabetes. This study suggests that even with the genetic predisposition, type 2 diabetes could be prevented with a healthy diet.

LIKE AN ONION

The link between lifestyle and genes has been proven by scientists and doctors over and over again. Even when someone has all the genes that lead to type 2 diabetes, the expression of these genes can be partially offset by a healthy environment. That means eating a low fat diet and getting plenty of exercise. The Pima Indians who developed diabetes and then changed their lifestyle were often able to lose weight and decrease insulin resistance, and thus kept their diabetes under control. This is the ultimate goal of all genetic researchers—to prevent, control, or cure diabetes.

But as diabetes expert David Mendosa says, "Trying to understand diabetes is like peeling an onion. Not only do both activities tend to make us cry, but also as soon as we reach one layer, there's another one to cut through."[21]

7

GENE THERAPY FOR DIABETES

Gene therapy is using DNA technology to prevent, control, or cure disease. Often this means altering genes or the way the genes are expressed. It means genetic engineering on the human level instead of just with bacteria or human insulin. Gene therapy is so new that most efforts at treatment are still experimental, but the hope of scientists who search for diabetes genes is to be able to alter those genes and someday permanently prevent or cure diabetes.

GENES AS WARNING SIGNS

The first hope of scientists is to use their knowledge of genetic risk to prevent diabetes from developing or at least to delay its onset. The scientists at ChemGenex want to do just that with their discovery of the PSARL gene. They are working on a DNA test that can be used to pinpoint the PSARL gene in obese people. Any DNA analysis that shows evidence of a variation in the PSARL gene will indicate a person at high risk for type 2 diabetes. Although this knowledge would not be a treatment, it would be a warning to the people with positive results. They would have strong evidence that diabetes was in their future if they did not change their lifestyle. Knowledge of the risk would encourage people to work to lose weight, eat a healthy diet, and get enough exercise. Long before insulin resistance or diabetes developed, the risk could be diagnosed. ChemGenex scientists believe that a PSARL gene test could delay or prevent type 2 diabetes. The test is neither easy nor inexpensive yet. Even though scientists have sequenced the whole human genome, they are not used to having to identify a variation in just one gene. ChemGenex, however, predicts it will have such a test by about 2009. If they do, it will be the first genetic test for type 2 diabetes, and it may help prevent the disease in vulnerable people.

GENE MARKERS AND INTERVENTION

A team of scientists in Italy tried to prevent type 1 diabetes by identifying genetic markers of risk, too. They concentrated on HLA genes that seem to cause immune system attacks. Between 1999 and 2002, the team tested newborn babies and selected those with the HLA variations that increase risk for type 1 diabetes. Then, they set up an experiment to see if early use of cow's milk causes the development of the autoantibodies that often lead to diabetes. The study was named PREVEFIN. The scientists checked the babies for two years. Those who were bottle fed were given extra vitamin D. Vitamin D is believed to have a protective effect for beta cells. Also, these babies were fed a formula made from a special cow's milk that did not contain casein. Casein is the protein that scientists suspect may cause antibodies to develop in vulnerable children. It is the foreign food protein typically encountered first by infants. After two years, the PREVEFIN scientists tested the children for the antibodies that are always found before type 1 diabetes begins. Breastfed babies had no antibodies to beta cells, and babies that drank the special cow's milk did not develop beta cell autoantibodies as often as babies who drink regular cow's milk. The scientists suspected that they may have prevented some cases of diabetes, but the study was too small to know for sure.

The NIH, along with diabetes organizations in several nations, began a worldwide study of PREVEFIN's findings in 2002. The study is called TRIGR. It is the Trial to Reduce IDDM (insulin-dependent diabetes mellitus) in the Genetically at Risk. Thousands of children with HLA markers for increased risk are being followed for years. Mothers are encouraged to breastfeed, but those who do not are provided with the special milk formulas that reduce the chance of antibodies developing. By study's end, TRIGR scientists will have an answer to a major question about type 1 diabetes. They will know if early exposure to cow's milk triggers the genes that cause diabetes. Perhaps they will have a proven way to prevent type 1 diabetes in children at genetic risk.

Preventing or delaying diabetes by diagnosing genetic risk is exciting, but there is still not a therapy that cures diabetes once it has developed. Scientists are determined to find a gene therapy that can cure, but it is not easy. Therapy for type 2 diabetes will have to involve a cure for obesity and insulin resistance. Therapy for type 1 will need to concentrate on insulin production and the immune system.

PANCREATIC TRANSPLANTS

Doctors and scientists have already succeeded in replacing destroyed beta cells in some type 1 diabetics. Just as doctors perform heart or kidney transplants, they can perform pancreatic transplants to cure or improve type 1 diabetes. As with other transplants, they use donor organs. The trouble is that there are few donor pancreases available compared to the number of people who would benefit. Also, the surgery is dangerous and difficult. Most doctors refuse to do these transplants unless the person has developed kidney damage so severe that a kidney is also needed. About 1,500 such transplants are performed every year, but even these transplants do not come without complications. The immune system recognizes the foreign pancreas as an invader to be attacked. Therefore, strong drugs to suppress the immune system are required for life.

A newer kind of transplant is called the Edmonton Protocol, after the city where it was developed in Canada. In this procedure, only islet cells of the pancreas are transplanted. Doctors retrieve these islet cells from a donor pancreas and place them in the diabetic person's liver. Because diabetes damages or destroys a diabetic person's pancreas, the beta cells are transplanted into the liver, where they begin to work to produce insulin. The operation is easy and safe. Dan Quigley, who lives in Wisconsin, had this operation in 2002. The islet cells he received did make insulin but not enough. Quigley had two more transplants of the cells in 2003 and 2004. After the last transplant, Quigley became one of the few people in the world cured of his type 1 diabetes. He no longer needed insulin shots at all. He could eat ice cream. He could stop worrying about testing his blood sugar levels. He was 14 years old when he developed diabetes. Suddenly, in his mid-50s, he was not diabetic anymore. Quigley and his doctors were very happy with his results, but no one can say how long they will last.[22]

Fewer than half the people who get islet cell transplants are able to stop using insulin shots for life. Even when the procedure is successful, the transplanted beta cells do not produce enough insulin to cure the diabetes long term. Most people need to go back to injecting insulin within 2 years. The Edmonton Procedure works well, but most people are improved, not cured. Furthermore, the procedure is

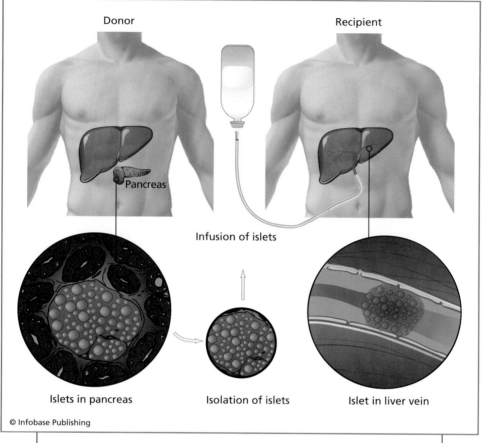

Donor

Recipient

Pancreas

Infusion of islets

Islets in pancreas

Isolation of islets

Islet in liver vein

© Infobase Publishing

FIGURE 7.1 In the Edmonton Protocol, islet cells are surgically removed from the pancreas of a donor organ, checked for good health, and purified. The islets are transplanted with a long needle into a vein that serves the patient's liver. The cells travel to the liver and begin producing insulin.

complicated and very expensive. Not enough donor pancreases are available. Half of the pancreas's 1 million cells are needed for each transplant. If the transplants are ever to be used regularly to cure type 1 diabetes, many more cells would have to be available. Also, just as with pancreas transplants, the procedure can cause problems for the immune system. Patients have to take drugs to suppress immune system recognition of the transplanted cells as foreign invaders to be attacked. They must also take drugs to stop the formation of autoantibodies against beta cells, which was what caused the diabetes in the first place. These drugs have serious side effects. Some people feel so sick from the drugs that they stop taking them. When the drugs are stopped, their immune system destroys the new beta cells just as it did the old ones.

TRANSPLANTS WITH GENE THERAPY

Some scientists are experimenting with gene therapy to try to overcome the problems with islet cell transplants and autoimmune attacks. So far, their experiments have been with NOD mice or rats, not people, but the gene therapy has been remarkably successful. At the University of Pittsburgh, Andrew Stewart led a scientific team that used a virus to alter the genes in rats with type 1 diabetes. The procedure is similar to the recombinant DNA technology used to add a DNA sequence to a bacterium. Instead of adding DNA codes to a bacterium, however, the Pittsburgh team added the genetic material to a virus.

Viruses are able to carry their genes into other living cells and then to force the invaded cells to use their own viral DNA as instructions. This is how viruses grow and reproduce. It is how they cause disease in plants and animals, including people. In the laboratory, scientists can cut and paste the viruses' genes so that they are harmless. Then, they can add useful genes or DNA sequences to the virus using recombinant DNA technology. When the altered virus is injected into rat cells, for example, the virus adds the new therapeutic DNA to the rat's cells. The virus is a carrier, or vector, for getting the new DNA instruction into living cells. The cells now carry the information to code for healthy functioning. This technology is very new and has not yet resulted in many treatments. The Pittsburgh team, however, was able to use the technology to help diabetic rats grow new beta cells.

The Pittsburgh team used an adenovirus for their work. Adenoviruses usually cause illnesses like colds and eye infections. First, the scientists cut out the part of the viral DNA code that makes animals sick. Then, they added a DNA sequence that codes for HGF. HGF is a growth factor. It instructs beta cells to multiply by cell division. It also seems to help beta cells to live longer. The scientists injected the altered viruses into islet cells taken from the pancreases of healthy rats. Then, they injected these islet cells, with their HGF viral instructions, into the livers of rats with type 1 diabetes. They gave the diabetic rats drugs to suppress immune system responses to the foreign islet cells. This procedure was just like the Edmonton Protocol for transplanting healthy islet cells from donors into people with type 1 diabetes.

HOW THE RATS RESPONDED

The new beta cells immediately began to make insulin in the diabetic rats. The rats' blood sugars dropped. Their glucose levels were much better than the levels achieved in rats that received islet cell transplants without the HGF gene. What was especially exciting was how long the islet cells survived and kept working. They lasted twice as long as islet cells without the HGF gene. For 18 weeks, the rats' glucose level stayed 200 mg/dl below the glucose levels of rats that did not receive the gene transfer. The Pittsburgh scientists think they have found an excellent way to improve islet transplants for people. Since rats live only two years, 18 weeks for them is the equivalent of 10 years for people. With HGF gene therapy, fewer donor cells would be needed for islet transplants, and the beta cells would last longer, perhaps keeping people from needing insulin shots for a decade.

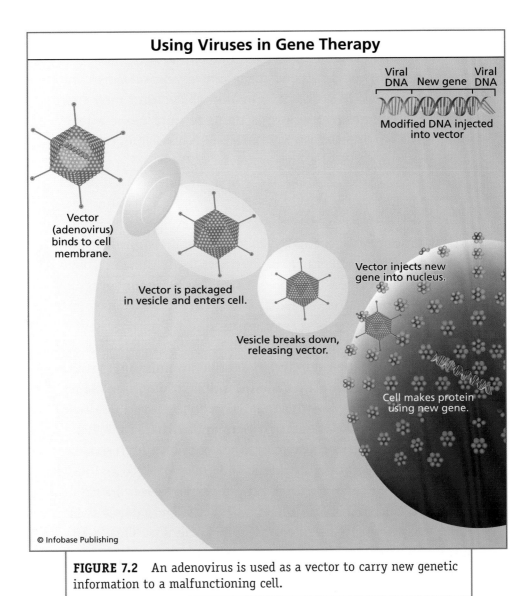

Using Viruses in Gene Therapy

Viral DNA   New gene   Viral DNA

Modified DNA injected into vector

Vector (adenovirus) binds to cell membrane.

Vector is packaged in vesicle and enters cell.

Vesicle breaks down, releasing vector.

Vector injects new gene into nucleus.

Cell makes protein using new gene.

© Infobase Publishing

FIGURE 7.2   An adenovirus is used as a vector to carry new genetic information to a malfunctioning cell.

However, the Pittsburgh scientists also discovered a major problem. They tested the drugs that stop the immune system from attacking transplanted cells in normal, healthy rats. These rats all developed severe diabetes and died. Stewart looked at these results and worried that the same thing was happening in people who had to use the powerful drugs for islet cell transplants. Immune system drugs could be hurting islet cells. This could explain why islet cell transplants do not last. It could explain why most transplant patients needed to go back to insulin shots after only two years. If immune system drugs damage beta cells, a true cure for type 1 diabetes may have to involve gene therapy for the immune system.

GENE THERAPY FOR THE IMMUNE SYSTEM

A NOD mouse experiment by University of Pittsburgh scientist Khaleel Rehman Khaja might provide an answer. Khaja added a gene named IL-4 to a virus. IL-4 codes for proteins that make regulatory T cells. These are cells that regulate the immune system by suppressing its activity when needed. Khaja injected the virus into the beta cells of NOD mice. The IL-4 genes seemed to act like an immune system switch and prevented the mice from developing high blood glucose levels or hyperglycemia. The mice stayed healthy, and T cells did not attack their beta cells. Khaja believes a technique like this could also prevent people at high risk for type 1 from developing diabetes.

In 2006, Matthias von Herrath, an expert on type 1 diabetes, cured NOD mice of their diabetes by getting their immune systems to tolerate rather than attack beta cells. His approach combined two treatment approaches. He treated the mice with a kind of "anti-antibody" that calms down the immune system, and also added a vaccine that induces regulatory cells to protect the beta cells from T-cell attacks. His treatment did not work on all the mice, but most showed no signs of diabetes, even a year after the treatment. Herrath's treatment is already being tried in some tests of people with type 1 diabetes. His approach is very exciting because if it is successful, it could replace the need for insulin injections. If the studies are successful, gene therapy may become a reality for type 1 diabetes within a few years.

GENE THERAPY FOR TYPE 2

Gene therapy has also shown great promise in studies for type 2 diabetes. At the University of Florida, Satya Kalra led a scientific team that cured type 2 diabetes in obese mice. The team used a virus as a vector for the gene transfer of leptin, the hormone that controls appetite. Leptin acts in the hypothalamus, a special area of the brain, to control fullness or hunger. The hypothalamus responds to the leptin by turning appetite on or off. It also controls how much insulin is made in response to a rich diet. Usually, the hypothalamus reacts to high levels of leptin. It also prevents too much insulin production, even when a high-fat diet is eaten. In type 2 diabetic mice, however, this does not happen. The hypothalamus seems to be insensitive to the leptin. More and more insulin is produced, fat cells become insulin resistant, and pancreases are so overworked that beta cells give out.

Kalra's team injected the leptin gene directly into the brains of half the diabetic mice. Their hypothalamuses began to make leptin. Then the scientists fed all their mice a rich, high-fat diet. Leptin production was increased in all the treated mice. Even though they consumed a high-fat diet, which typically causes glucose and insulin levels to rise, their glucose and insulin levels became normal. The mice that did not get the gene therapy continued to have glucose and insulin levels that were too high. Kalra was also happy to discover that the mice producing extra leptin lived longer than the other mice, even though both groups were obese.

Kalra is doing more studies to be sure the gene therapy is safe and effective. He believes the treatment might help people someday. He says that just one shot might reverse diabetes. Gene therapy with animals suggests exciting pos-

DO WE REALLY WANT TO KNOW?

Someday, people will be able to know in advance whether they carry genes for diseases and whether they have passed those genes on to their unborn children. Then, many people predict, humanity will face a dilemma. Should fetuses carrying genes for diseases such as diabetes be aborted? Should people's genomes be reported to insurance companies when they carry a gene for a disease that is expensive to treat? Will our genes belong to us or be public information? Will we pass laws allowing only those with healthy genes to have children? And if a person had the gene for a deadly disease, would he or she want to know that a tragic death was coming? These are questions that many are concerned about.

The day may come when diseases such as diabetes can be cured with gene therapy, but that will also be the day when genes are so well understood that scientists will be able to manipulate them at will. They may not only be able to alter the genes in an embryo for good health, but also to select for beauty, intelligence, hair color, or straight teeth. What would be moral and who would decide? Questions like these create controversy whenever gene therapy is discussed. That is why, almost everywhere in the world, there are laws forbidding scientists from adding DNA to human embryos.

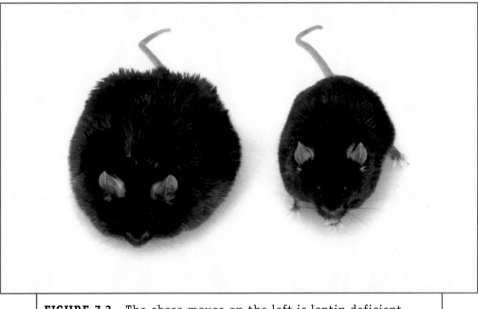

FIGURE 7.3 The obese mouse on the left is leptin deficient and cannot control its appetite. It grows more and more obese in comparison to a normal mouse (right) and is more likely to develop type 2 diabetes.

sibilities for human gene therapy in the future. Much work remains to be done, however, before there is a cure for diabetes in humans. Until all the genes that actually code for diabetes are known and isolated, developing complete gene therapies is just not possible. Some scientists wonder if the ultimate cure will rest in the healing power of human cells themselves in the form of **stem cells**, the specialized cells from which all other cells arise.

8

STEM CELLS: THE ULTIMATE CURE?

Many scientists believe that special body cells called stem cells could be the answer for the cure of many diseases, including type 1 and type 2 diabetes. Research with stem cells is very new, but stem cell scientists and people with untreatable, incurable diseases are strong supporters of stem cell research. The research being conducted today may be tomorrow's best treatments for diabetes.

STEM CELL CHARACTERISTICS

Stem cells are cells that can generate or develop into other cells. They are the cells that give rise to every cell in the body. Stem cells are organized factories, with nuclei and chromosomes, like other cells, but they have three very special properties. First, stem cells are **unspecialized**. This means that they do not have specialized functions, like muscle cells, nerve cells, or beta cells. However, these unspecialized cells have the ability to **differentiate** into new cells. Given the right chemical signals, stem cells can differentiate into functioning body cells with specific jobs. Stem cells also have the ability to **proliferate**. This means they are able to make more of themselves, to multiply by the millions without specializing. Because stem cells are unspecialized yet able to proliferate and differentiate, they are the very stuff of life. Without them, human beings would not develop. They are the process by which life begins.

TOTIPOTENT STEM CELLS

A zygote is really a super stem cell. The zygote splits into two cells, each with all the genetic information of the parent cell. The two cells divide again, becoming four and then eight. During these first few cell divisions, the cells are **totipotent** stem cells. Each cell is capable of giving rise to every cell needed to grow an embryo, a fetus, and then a newborn baby. At the next cell divisions, when there are 16 cells, totipotency is gone. The cells have already begun to slightly differentiate. By the fourth day of growth, the new life is a ball about 120 cells large. It is called a **blastocyst**. The outer layers of the blastocyst attach to the wall of the mother's uterus and eventually become the placenta and umbilical cord for the growing embryo. These are the baby's lifelines through which it receives food and oxygen from the mother's body.

PLURIPOTENT STEM CELLS

The inner cells of the blastocyst are **pluripotent** stem cells. These cells cannot differentiate into all the cells needed to grow a new life, such as the placenta, but they are capable of giving rise to any cell in the body. If the outer cells successfully implant in the uterus, the pluripotent stem cells of the blastocyst continue to multiply and then group together, form layers, and begin specializing into all the organs, tissues, and body parts of a growing embryo. By the time eight weeks have passed, the embryo is a fetus, and the pluripotent stem cells have disappeared. They have specialized into skin cells, brain cells, pancreatic cells, and all of the more than 200 kinds of cells that form the human body. Pluripotent stem cells are also called **embryonic stem cells** or ES

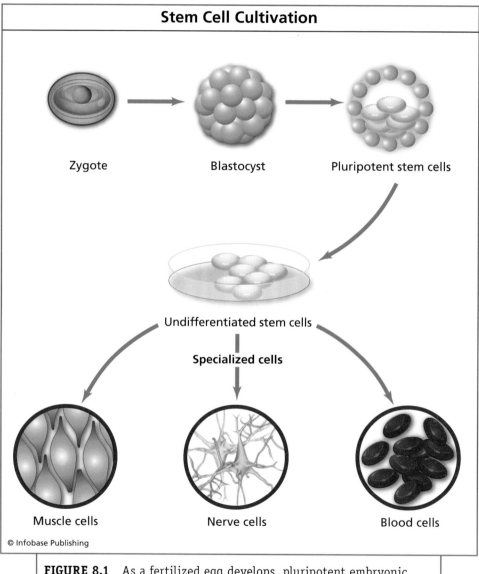

Stem Cell Cultivation

Zygote Blastocyst Pluripotent stem cells

Undifferentiated stem cells

Specialized cells

Muscle cells Nerve cells Blood cells

© Infobase Publishing

FIGURE 8.1 As a fertilized egg develops, pluripotent embryonic stem cells appear and develop into specialized body cells. Embryonic stem cells also can be removed from the blastocyst and grown into many specialized cells in the lab.

cells. They exist only in the embryo, to grow the fetus, and are gone long before the baby is born.

MULTIPOTENT STEM CELLS

Some stem cells, however, remain in body organs, even after birth. They are unspecialized and able to proliferate and differentiate, but they are not as flexible as pluripotent stem cells. These are the **multipotent** stem cells. They cannot give rise to every cell in the body, but they can regenerate cells in the organs where they are found. These multipotent cells are called **adult stem cells**, or AS cells, for short. Some remain very active in the body during an individual's entire life. Skin, for example, has a lot of stem cells because it is often damaged and requires repair. When skin is slashed or burned, the damaged cells send emergency chemical signals to the resting stem cells. The adult skin stem cells "wake up" in response and begin to divide. Each cell gives rise to two daughter cells. One daughter cell specializes into a skin cell and moves to the area of the wound. The other remains unspecialized. Since adult stem cells divide like this, injuries are repaired and the skin never loses its population of adult stem cells. They return to a resting state until they are signaled again. Adult stem cells in the skin cannot differentiate into heart cells or brain cells, but they can continue to give rise to all the skin cells that are needed.

Many organs of the body are equipped with their own adult stem cells. Bone marrow, for instance, has stem cells that can produce any kind of blood or bone cell. To the surprise of scientists, however, other organs have adult stem cells that do not seem to do anything. The stem cells in the eyes, brain, and heart, for example, stay in a resting state, even when the organs are damaged. Pancreatic stem cells were not even discovered until 2004, and they, too, seem to stay at rest instead of replacing damaged beta

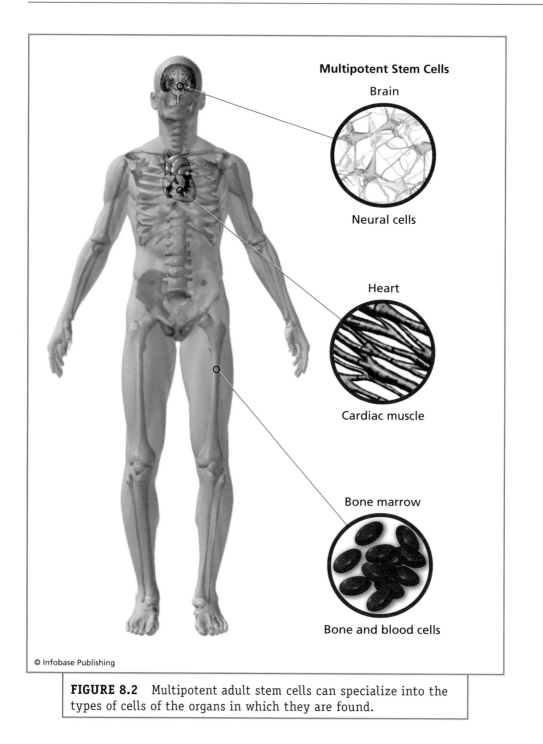

Multipotent Stem Cells

Brain

Neural cells

Heart

Cardiac muscle

Bone marrow

Bone and blood cells

© Infobase Publishing

FIGURE 8.2 Multipotent adult stem cells can specialize into the types of cells of the organs in which they are found.

cells. Stem cell scientists around the world are experimenting with adult stem cells to see if they can be persuaded to wake up, turn on, and heal injuries or grow new body cells. There have been some exciting successes with animals, but for diabetes, as well as many other severe diseases, adult stem cells do not seem to be the answer for most scientists. Embryonic stem cells, with their flexibility, pluripotency, and ability to differentiate into any body cell, seem to hold the most promise for cures.

ES CELLS IN THE LAB

Scientists can remove embryonic stem cells from the blastocysts of animals or people and grow them in their laboratories. In the case of humans, the ES cells are retrieved from the unwanted and often discarded zygotes stored at in vitro fertilization clinics. These are zygotes formed in lab petri dishes for couples who have trouble conceiving. In vitro clinics usually prepare several fertilized eggs that are not implanted in the mother's uterus. They are extras, in case the first efforts at pregnancy do not work. With the couple's permission, these are the zygotes used by stem cell scientists.

The zygotes are grown to the blastocyst stage in a special nutrient bath in petri dishes. Then the ES cells are moved to new petri dishes, where they are bathed in a chemical "soup" that encourages them to divide and grow. Scientists are able to grow millions of ES cells this way and to keep them alive indefinitely. The cells can be encouraged to differentiate into different body cells with other nutrient chemicals. These **stem cell lines** are the raw material with which scientists believe they will someday cure many diseases, including diabetes.

Growing stem cell lines in the laboratory is tricky. They have to be kept proliferating and yet not allowed to clump together and start to differentiate. Finding the exact combination of nutrients to make them differentiate into the desired cells is even harder. To make each stem cell line specialize into specific kinds of body cells takes a different nutrient bath. Usually, scientists first learn to make the ES cells specialize as they wish with animals.

ES CELLS TO BETA CELLS

In 2006, a stem cell company called Novocell, was able to use human ES cells to make beta cells in the laboratory. Novocell scientists invented a chemical coating that encapsulates the cells. This coating could solve the immune system problem with type 1 diabetes by protecting the cells from attack by T cells. The cells stay alive and are able to produce insulin.

JUST GROW A NEW PANCREAS

Anthony Atala is a tissue engineering scientist at Wake Forest University. He uses the body's adult stem cells to try to grow new body tissues and organs in his lab. He takes cells, places them on a mold in the laboratory, and gives them the right nutrients to specialize and multiply. The cells form tissue that grows into the right shape because of the mold. Then he implants the organ or tissue back into the body from which the cells came. Atala grew bladders for dogs in 1999 and implanted them back into the dogs, where they worked normally. He has grown blood vessels, muscles, and a uterus for other animals. In 2006, he and his colleagues reported growing partial bladders for seven young people who could not urinate normally. The laboratory bladders

Novocell is currently studying how encapsulated beta cells work in people. For this study, they encapsulated beta cells from organ donors. Volunteers have received injections of the cells. They are checked every month to be sure the coatings are safe for people. Their insulin levels are also checked to see if the transplanted cells are producing insulin. If the study is a success, Novocell hopes that the discovery will make it easy to replace islet cells for people with type 1 diabetes.

In an animal study in 2008, Novocell reported more evidence that ES cells hold great promise for treating type 1 diabetes. Novocell scientists grew pancreatic cells from human embryonic stem cells in their lab and injected these cells into 105 NOD mice. The cells lived, began making insulin in the diabetic mice, and controlled their blood glucose levels. After about three months, the scientists removed the injected cells, and the mice immediately demonstrated

did not cure the young people, but they were much improved. Tissue engineering is an exciting new science with wonderful future possibilities.

Atala and his scientific team are currently working on learning to grow pancreas tissue. Atala knows that it will be many years before scientists can regenerate any organ to replace a diseased one, but he is confident that it will happen someday. He points to the ability of animals like the lizard, which can grow a new tail, and the octopus, which can regenerate an arm. Why cannot people get new body parts, too? If Atala's tissue engineering dream comes true, diabetes could be cured with new pancreases grown in the lab whenever they were needed.

a sharp rise in blood sugar. This proved that it was the embryonic stem cells "grown up" into beta cells that had successfully prevented diabetes in the mice.

Such ES cell breakthroughs are exciting, but they have not yet been used as a treatment for people, and researchers are not sure that such treatments will be safe. Many scientists worry that stem cells could interfere with normal functioning of the body's other cells. Others are concerned that stem cells introduced into bodies might keep proliferating and cause cancers. In the Novocell study, for example, 7 of the 105 treated mice developed tumors. Much more research is needed to understand why the tumors occurred and how to prevent them. Studies with animals must continue before ES cell treatments become a reality for people.

ES CELLS AND THERAPEUTIC CLONING

The ES cell technology that many scientists think could actually cure diabetes in the future is called **therapeutic cloning**. It is a way to make stem cell lines that are a perfect genetic match to any person. So far, no one has used it with humans, but scientists know just how it would work in theory. The first step would be to take a body cell, perhaps a skin cell, from a patient. This cell's nucleus carries all the genetic information unique to that person. The nucleus is removed from the cell and placed inside an enucleated egg. An enucleated egg is one with its nucleus removed. The egg,

(opposite) **FIGURE 8.3** Therapeutic cloning involves taking an egg from which the nucleus has been removed, and replacing that nucleus with DNA from the cell of another organism. The result is a blastocyst with almost identical DNA to the original organism.

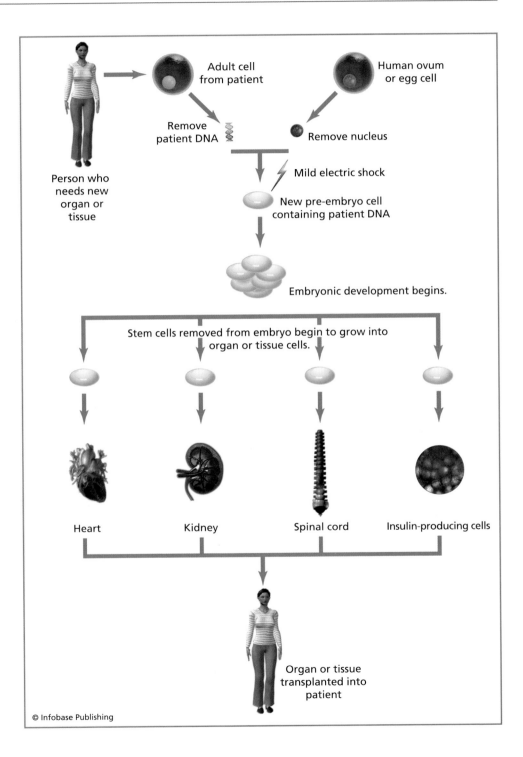

Adult cell from patient

Human ovum or egg cell

Remove patient DNA

Remove nucleus

Person who needs new organ or tissue

Mild electric shock

New pre-embryo cell containing patient DNA

Embryonic development begins.

Stem cells removed from embryo begin to grow into organ or tissue cells.

Heart

Kidney

Spinal cord

Insulin-producing cells

Organ or tissue transplanted into patient

with the new nucleus, would be encouraged to divide and grow into a blastocyst. (This can be done without fertilization by a sperm; a chemical or electrical stimulation is used to start the growth.) Once the blastocyst is grown, its stem cells would be removed and grown into a stem cell line in the lab. The stem cells could now be differentiated into beta cells or any cells, each an exact genetic match to the patient who gave the skin cell. The beta cells would now be available as a treatment that would not be attacked by the body's immune system. The treatment could be repeated every year or so, keeping the patient healthy and normal for life.

THE MORAL DILEMMA OF STEM CELLS

Scientists can imagine unlimited future stem cell treatments, and many have already been successful with animal tests. They predict that stem cells will revolutionize medicine and make diabetes a disease of the past. When, or even if, this will happen, however, is not certain. Many thoughtful people are opposed to human embryonic stem cell research. Embryonic stem cell research means destroying an embryo, and people who are opposed believe this means killing some lives in order to save others.

Many are also opposed to the use of therapeutic cloning techniques. The process of therapeutic cloning is the same that has been used to clone animals. Theoretically, humans could be cloned if the egg were placed in a uterus to grow instead of being grown to the blastocyst stage and used in the lab. Almost no one believes such reproductive cloning is either safe or moral. Stem cell scientists say cloning a human being is too dangerous. Too often in animals the attempts lead to death for the baby and the mother. They argue that therapeutic cloning has a much different goal than reproductive cloning, but the opponents are not convinced. Stem cell scientists argue that their research is moral and will someday alleviate the suffering of millions of people already born. Their research, however, is made difficult by current U.S. policies.

In the United States, no one prevents or outlaws human ES cell research, but the government currently does not support it with federal funds. Thus, ES cell research in the United States is either privately or state supported. For example, in 2004, the state of California passed a bond measure that offers $3 billion of state money to scientists who are doing embryonic stem cell research. This policy was approved by voters who believe in the promise for cures of diseases such as diabetes. Around the world, human ES cell research is outlawed in some countries but supported in others. Human ES cell research is a controversy with no easy answers.

ADULT STEM CELLS

Adult stem cells (AS cells) do not cause the same controversy as embryonic stem cells. Many scientists believe AS cells hold great promise for future cures. However, AS cells are more difficult to work with than ES cells. They are difficult to isolate from body organs and hard to grow and keep alive in petri dishes. It has proven difficult to find the right chemical signals to get them to turn on, wake up, and heal injuries. Nevertheless, scientists are overcoming the difficulties.

In 2006, Darwin Prockop succeeded in treating mice with type 2 diabetes using adult stem cells. Prockop used mice specially bred to have weak immune systems. He did not use adult stem cells from the pancreas, but instead used adult stem cells from human bone marrow because the cells are already turned on and active. The human stem cells did not kill the special mice because their immune systems were too weak to attack the foreign cells. He injected these stem cells into his mice. Usually, these stem cells would make only blood or bone cells, but Prockop discovered that the treated mice made more insulin. He found stem cells in the mouse pancreas and kidneys. This was especially good news because kidneys are so often damaged by diabetes. The AS cells seemed to be repairing damage in both organs. Prockop thinks AS cell treatments could help people with type 2 diabetes. His study is the first of its kind, so much

SUPPORTERS OF EMBRYONIC STEM CELL RESEARCH

Diabetes is not the only serious disease or injury that might be cured someday with embryonic stem cells. Actor Michael J. Fox, for instance, has Parkinson's disease and is a very strong supporter of embryonic stem cell research. His Michael J. Fox Foundation for Parkinson's Research bestows grants to scientists doing embryonic stem cell research that could lead to medical treatments. Nancy Reagan, the wife of former president Ronald Reagan, is another supporter of stem cell research. Ronald Reagan died of Alzheimer's disease, and Nancy Reagan thinks that embryonic stem cells might lead to a cure for this cruel disease. Most people in the United States agree with Fox and Reagan. In 2007, an ABC News/*Washington Post* poll revealed that 61% of Americans support embryonic stem cell research. In June 2007, the *Washington Post* surveyed 1,020 couples who have extra embryos stored in in vitro clinics, and 60% of them said they would like to donate these embryos for stem cell research.

more research with animals has to be done. But his results are very encouraging. If stem cells could be taken from a person's own bone marrow to treat diabetes, no immune system attacks would occur. Scientists have discovered that a few bone marrow stem cells, perhaps 1% to 3%, can sometimes specialize into cells for other organs. In labs around the country, they are following up on Prockop's discovery and trying to treat other animals with bone marrow stem cells. If they succeed, a treatment for type 2 diabetes may be close.

THE HOPE OF THE FUTURE

Scientists continue to research both adult stem cells and embryonic stem cells in their search for a cure for diabetes. They explore the possibility of gene therapies combined with therapeutic cloning to completely prevent autoimmune type 1 attacks. It would be just a matter of adding the DNA sequence that signals "self" to the stem cell line. Many scientists believe that success will come during the lifetime of young people today, but no one knows from which kind of stem cell the answer will come. That is why stem cell scientists insist that investigating both types of stem cells is necessary. They believe that they will be able to help the millions of people with diabetes live normal, healthy lives. They have faith in the promise of stem cell research and predict that in time, diabetes will finally be conquered.

NOTES

1. "Amanda" (Published Dec. 18, 2005), Kids' Voices, Children with Diabetes, http://www.childrenwithdiabetes.com/kids/d_02_1sm.htm.

2. "Kassy" (Published July 22, 2003), Kids' Voices, Children with Diabetes, http://www.childrenwithdiabetes.com/kids/d_02_1np.htm.

3. "Daniel," Kids' Voices, Children with Diabetes, http://www.childrenwithdiabetes.com/kids/d_02_1a6.htm (accessed Jan. 5, 2007).

4. Bonnie Siegler, "Halle Berry: My Battle with Diabetes," *Daily Mail*, December 14, 2005, http://www.dailymail.co.uk/pages/live/articles/health/healthmain.html?in_article_id=371528&in_page_id=1774.

5. Danielle Kazista, e-mail communication with author, November 7, 2006.

6. NBC10.Com Health Encyclopedia, "Patti LaBelle Kicking Diabetes 'In the Butt,'" October 28, 2004, http://www.nbc10.com/health/3871037/detail.html.

7. University of Kentucky Health and Medical Science News, "Franklin County Boy to Be Featured During Annual Children's Miracle Network Celebration to Benefit Kentucky Children's Hospital," June 15, 2006, http://www.uky.edu/PR/News/CMN/2006CMN-Franklin_County_Boy.htm.

8. Quoted in Lee J. Sanders, DPM, "From Thebes to Toronto and the 21st Century: An Incredible Journey," *Diabetes Spectrum*, June, 2001, http://spectrum.diabetesjournals.org/cgi/content/full/15/1/56?maxtoshow=&HITS=10&hits=10&RESULTFORMAT=&author1=sanders,+lee&searchid=1069902237963_203&stored_search=&FIRSTINDEX=0&sortspec=relevance&journalcode=diaspect.

9. Austin Bunn, "The Way We live Now: 3-16-03: Body Check; The Bittersweet Science," *New York Times* Magazine Desk, http://querry.nytimes.com/gst/fullpage.html?sec=health&res=9F0

CE6DC143EF935A25750C0A 9659C8B63 (accessed January 7, 2007).

10. Joan MacCracken, MD, "From Ants to Analogues: Puzzles and Promises in Diabetes Management," *Postgraduate MedicineOnline*, 101 (1997), http:// www.postgradmed. com/issues/1997/04_97/ diabetes.htm.

11. Quoted in Bunn, "The Way We Live Now: 3-16-03: Body Check; The Bittersweet Science."

12. Kazista, e-mail communication with author.

13. Henry Gee, *Jacob's Ladder: The History of the Human Genome.* New York: W.W. Norton and Company, 2004, pp. 149–152.

14. James D. Watson with Andrew Berry, *DNA: The Secret of Life*. New York: Alfred A. Knopf, 2003, pp. 15–16.

15. Watson, *DNA: The Secret of Life*. New York: Alfred A. Knopf, 2003, pp. 88 and 91.

16. P.J. Bingley, E.A. Gale, "Progression to Type 1 Diabetes in Islet Cell antibody-positive Relatives in the European Nicotinamide Diabetes Intervention Trial: The Role of Additional Immune, Genetic, and Metabolic Markers of Risk," *Diabetologia* 49 (2006): 881–890, (reprinted in NCBI: PubMed), http://www.ncbi. nlm.nih.gov/entrez/query. fcgi?cmd=Retrieve&db=Pub Med&list_uids=16514546&d opt=Abstract.

17. Quoted in American Chemical Society, "Chemists Identify Key Gene in Development of Type 1 Diabetes," April 7, 2005, *Science Daily*, http://www. sciencedaily.com/releases/ 2005/03/050325230349.htm.

18. Quoted in Toni Baker, "Worldwide Study Looks to Find Causes of Type 1 Diabetes," Feb. 13, 2006, Medical College of Georgia: Science/Medical News, http://www.mcg.edu/news/ 2006NewsRel/She021306. html.

19. Quoted in Jeff Wheelwright, "Native America's Alleles," *Discover Magazine* 26 (2005), http://www. discover.com/issues/ may-05/features/native-americas-alleles/?page=1.

20. Quoted in "A Mother and Her Daughters," The Pima Indians, http://diabetes. niddk.nih.gov/dm/pubs/ pima/mother/mother.htm.

21. David Mendosa, "Diabetes Genes," August 17, 2005, http://www.mendosa.com/ genes.htm.

22. Kawanza L. Griffin, "Cell Transplants at UW–Madison

Free Diabetic from Daily Insulin," *Milwaukee Journal Sentinel*, October 30, 2004, http://www.findarticles. com/p/articles/mi_qn4196/ is_20041030/ai_n11001891.

GLOSSARY

Adult stem cells   The stem cells that are present in the body after birth and can regenerate cells for the organs in which they are found. Adult stem cells are multipotent.

Amino acid   One of the building blocks of a protein. There are about 80 amino acids in nature, and the human body needs 20 of them to grow and maintain correct metabolism.

Antibodies   Proteins made by the body as part of the immune system. They recognize foreign invaders and begin an immune system attack.

Autoantibodies   Antibodies made by the immune system that are mistakenly directed against a part of the body. In type 1 diabetes, autoantibodies are made against the insulin-producing beta cells of the pancreas.

Autoimmune   A disordered response of the body in which the immune system reacts to the body's own tissue as if it is foreign.

Beta cells   Cells that make insulin. They are in the islets in the pancreas.

Blastocyst   The stage of an embryo before it has implanted in the uterus. It is a ball between 30 and 150 cells large and consists of an outer layer of cells and an inner mass of pluripotent stem cells.

Blood glucose levels   The amount of sugar (glucose) in a certain amount of blood. It is usually measured as milligrams (mg) of glucose in a deciliter (dl) of blood.

Cells The basic units or building blocks of all living things. Cells are living, functioning structures that take in nutrients and oxygen and manufacture proteins. Human bodies are made of about 100 trillion cells.

Chromosomes Structures in the nuclei of cells that carry hereditary information in the form of genes. Each chromosome is formed of one continuous strand of DNA. Humans have 23 pairs of chromosomes.

Clone A replica or identical genetic copy of a cell, a DNA sequence, or a whole organism.

Cytoplasm Jelly-like fluid inside the cell membrane and surrounding its nucleus.

Differentiate Undergoing the process of a specialized cell, such as a beta cell.

DNA (deoxyribonucleic acid) The genetic material of cells that codes for all body structures and functions. DNA is a long, double-stranded spiraling molecule called a double helix.

Dominant Expressed as a trait in an individual even if only one copy of the gene is present.

Embryo In humans, the developing organism in the uterus from the time of fertilization until the eighth week of growth.

Embryonic stem (ES) cells Primitive, unspecialized, flexible cells in the blastocyst. ES cells are pluripotent and able to give rise to every cell that makes up a living body.

Endoplasmic reticulum A network within the cell that serves to transport material and is the site of protein synthesis.

Fetus In humans, the developing life from about the eighth week after fertilization until birth.

Gene The basic unit of heredity that consists of a specific sequence of DNA.

Genetic engineering   Using scientific tools and techniques to change the genes and DNA in a cell for the benefit of humans.

Glucose   A simple form of sugar and the body's main source of energy.

Hormone   A chemical made by one part of the body to regulate the functioning of another part of the body.

Hyperglycemia   An undesirably high blood glucose level.

Hypoglycemia   An undesirably low blood glucose level.

Immune system   The complicated body system that fights off diseases and foreign material. It is a system of many components, including several kinds of white blood cells such as T cells.

Insulin   A hormone produced by the beta cells of the pancreas that helps the body use glucose for energy.

Insulin receptors   Substances on the outer parts of cells that bind with insulin, unlocking the cell so that glucose can enter.

Insulin resistance   The inability of cells to respond to insulin properly. The cells resist the insulin, making it difficult for glucose to enter. Insulin resistance seems to be worsened by fat in the cells. Insulin resistance leads to type 2 diabetes.

Introns   DNA segments within genes with poorly understood functions. They are non-coding parts of the gene that lie between the DNA coding sequences of the gene.

Messenger RNA (mRNA)   RNA that reads the code of a gene's DNA and carries the message to the transfer RNA.

Metabolic rate   The rate, or speed, at which food is converted into energy.

Mitochondria   The organelles that convert nutrients and oxygen into the energy to fuel the cell's activities. They are termed the powerhouses of the cell.

Multipotent   Able to give rise to the cells in a certain organ, but not all the cells of a body. Adult stem cells are multipotent.

Mutation   A permanent change, or variation, in DNA that is similar to a typographical error. Mutations are the cause of many inherited diseases.

Nucleus   The central part of the cell that carries the genetic material, or DNA.

Organelles   The structures of a cell that have specialized functions.

Pancreas   The organ in the body that makes insulin and digestive enzymes.

Penetrance   The degree to which a genetic trait is manifested. If only 50% of people with certain gene variations develop a trait or disease, the penetrance is 50%.

Plasmids   Circular pieces of DNA outside the chromosome of bacterial cells. They are not essential to the cell's functioning, but they can replicate themselves during cell division and be passed on to the daughter cells.

Pluripotent   Able to give rise to every kind of body cell, but not to the supporting fetal structures, such as the placenta. Embryonic stem cells are pluripotent.

Proliferate   Multiply and replicate, as in the division of stem cells into daughter cells.

Recessive   Expressed as a trait only if two copies of the gene are present. The opposite of dominant.

Recombinant DNA   A DNA sequence made artificially, usually in the laboratory, which joins two distinct pieces of DNA and forms a new sequence. Recombinant DNA is a process used to change the genetic structure of an organism.

Recombination The crossing over and shuffling of various alleles in chromosomes that results in a unique genetic arrangement for each new individual.

Regulator gene A gene that turns other genes off and on.

Restriction enzymes Proteins that recognize specific DNA sequences and cut them at those sites.

Ribosomes Cellular organelles that are the place where protein synthesis takes place.

RNA (ribonucleic acid) A nucleic acid that is similar to DNA, but is single stranded rather than double stranded and has a U for one chemical base instead of a T. It is involved in protein synthesis.

Stem cells Undifferentiated, flexible cells that are able to give rise to or differentiate into specialized cells.

Stem cell lines Embryonic stem cells that proliferate and stay alive for months or years in a petri dish without specializing in any way.

Therapeutic cloning Transfer of a cell's nucleus to an enucleated cell for the purposes of medical treatment. From this created cell, a stem cell line can be grown that is genetically identical to the person from whom the nucleus was taken and that can be used for medical therapy.

Totipotent Able to specialize into all cell types. Only the first few cell divisions of the zygote are totipotent.

Transfer RNA (tRNA) RNA that reads the messenger RNA code in groups of three and enables the ribosome to make amino acids.

Type 1 diabetes An autoimmune disease that leads to death of beta cells and high amounts of glucose in the blood. The body can produce little or no insulin in type 1 diabetes.

Type 2 diabetes A disease characterized by high amounts of glucose in the blood caused by the body's failure to produce enough insulin or to use the insulin it does produce. Type 2 diabetes is characterized by insulin resistance.

Unspecialized Without the ability to perform a specific body function; a property of stem cells. However, unspecialized stem cells can give rise to specialized cells.

Zygote A fertilized egg.

BIBLIOGRAPHY

"About Recombinant DNA." ThinkQuest Library. Available online. URL: http://library.thinkquest.org/04apr/00217/en/products/recdna/about.html.

Altman, Lawrence K. "The Tumultuous Discovery of Insulin: Finally, Hidden Story Is Told," *New York Times*, September 14, 1982. Available online. URL: http://query.nytimes.com/gst/fullpage.html?sec=health&res=9802E1D71238F937A25 75AC0A964948260.

"Aussies' Diabetes 'Saviour,'" *Sunday Times*, June 6, 2006, International Diabetes Institute. Available online. URL: http://www.diabetes.com.au/about.php?regionID=279.

Baker, Toni. "Journey of Hope: Worldwide Study Seeks Causes of Type 1 Diabetes," Medical College of Georgia, February 13, 2006. Available online. URL: http://cmbi.bjmu.edu.cn/news/0602/23.htm.

Bergeron, Bryan, MD. *Case Studies in Genes and Disease: A Primer for Clinicians.* Philadelphia: American College of Physicians, 2004.

Bernstein, Richard K. *Dr. Bernstein's Diabetes Solution Revised and Updated.* New York: Little Brown and Company, 2003.

Bunn, Austen. "The Way We Live Now: 3-16-03: Body Check; The Bittersweet Science," *New York Times* Magazine Desk. March 3, 2003. Available online. URL: http://query.nytimes.com/gst/fullpage.html?sec=health&res=9F0CE6DC143EF9 35A25750C0A9659C8B63.

"Centuries-old Epidemic Holds Clues to Today's Diabetes Puzzle, Says UCLA Study," News About the College, June 4, 2003.

UCLA Web site. Available online. URL: http://www.college. ucla.edu/news/03/diabetes.html.

"ChemGenex Discovery Highlighted at International Diabetes Conference," ChemGenex Pharmaceuticals. Available online. URL: http://www.chemgenex.com/wt/page/ pr_1149733195.

"Chemists Identify Key Gene in Development of Type 1 Diabetes," April 7, 2005, *ScienceDaily* Web site. Available online. URL: http://www.sciencedaily.com/releases/2005/03/0503 25230349.htm.

"Clinical Trial Shows Islet Transplantation Is a Promising Procedure for Certain Patients with Severe Type 1 Diabetes," Sept. 27, 2006, NIH News. Available online. URL: http:// www.nih.gov/news/pr/sep2006/niaid-27b.htm.

Clinical Trials, Novocell Web site. Available online. URL: http:// www.novocell.com/trials/.

Dean, Laura, M.D., and Joanna McEntyre, Ph.D. *The Genetic Landscape of Diabetes,* NCBI Web Site. Available online. URL: http://www.ncbi.nlm.nih.gov/books/bv.fcgi?rid=diabetes.

DeMouy, Jane. "The Pima Indians: Pathfinders for Health." NIDDK Web Site. Available online. URL: http://diabetes. niddk.nih.gov/dm/pubs/pima/pathfind/pathfind.htm.

"Diabetes Epidemic Could Wipe Out Indigenous Peoples: Experts," 2006, Physorg.com. URL: http://www.physorg. com/pdf82607698.pdf.

"Diabetes Mellitus, Insulin-Dependent; IDDM." Online Mendelian Inheritance of Man. NCBI Web site. Available online. URL: http://www.ncbi.nlm.nih.gov/entrez/dispomim. cgi?id=222100.

"DIPP." DIPP-TEDDY-TRIALNET. Avaliable online. URL: http:// research.utu.fi/dipp/index.php?page=RESEARCHPROJ: DIPP&lang=EN&city=TURKU.

"The Discovery of Insulin: A Canadian Medical Miracle of the 20th Century," Discovery of Insulin Web site. Available online. URL: http://www.discoveryofinsulin.com/Home. htm.

"GE In-Depth," Iowa Public Television. Available online. URL: http://www3.iptv.org/exploremore/ge/what/index.cfm.

Gee, Henry. *Jacob's Ladder.* New York: W.W. Norton & Company, 2004.

"Gene Therapy Prevents the Onset of Diabetic Symptoms in Mice," June 2, 2006, University of Pittsburgh Medical Center press release. Eureka Alert Web site. Available online. URL: http://www.eurekalert.org/pub_releases/2006-06/uopm-gtp053106.php.

"Gene Therapy Technique Reverses Type 2 Diabetes in Mice: Study Shows Promise of Leptin," September 21, 2006, *ScienceDaily* Web site. Available online. URL: http://www.sciencedaily.com/releases/2006/09/060920191021.htm.

Genetics Home Reference, Handbook. NIH Web site. Available online. URL: http://ghr.nlm.nih.gov/handbook;jsessionid= 415392F374450030378A80A91E2BDD48.

Goldberg, Carey. "Doctors Grow Bladder Cells and Produce Rebuilt Organ," *The Boston Globe*, April 4, 2006. Available online. URL: http://www.boston.com/yourlife/health/diseases/articles/2006/04/04/doctors_grow_bladder_cells_and_produce_rebuilt_organ/.

Goldberg, Daniella. "Cloning Around with Stem Cells," ABC Science Online. Available online. URL: http://abc.net.au/science/slab/stemcells/default.htm.

Griffin, Kawanza L. "Cell Transplants at UW-Madison Free Diabetic from Daily Insulin," *Milwaukee Journal Sentinel*, Oct. 30, 2004. Available online. URL: http://www.jsonline.com/story/index.aspx?id=270886.

"The History of Diabetes," Canadian Diabetes Association. Available online. URL: http://www.diabetes.ca/Section_About/timeline.asp.

Hitti, Miranda. "Adult Stem Cells May Treat Diabetes," Nov. 8, 2006, WebMD Health. Available online. URL: http://diabetes.webmd.com/news/20061108/adult-stem-cells-may-treat-diabetes.

Joslin Diabetes Center: Joslin Research Sections. Available online. URL: http://www.joslin.org/732_1206.asp.

"Kids' Voices." Children with Diabetes. Available online. URL: http://www.childrenwithdiabetes.com/kids/d_02_100.htm.

"Leslie J. Baier, Ph.D," NIDDK Web site. Available online. URL: http://intramural.niddk.nih.gov/research/faculty.asp?People_ID=1656.

MacCracken, Joan, M.D., with Donna Hoel. "From Ants to Analogues: Puzzles and Promises in Diabetes Management," PostGraduate Medicine Online 101 (1997). Available online. URL: http://www.postgradmed.com/issues/1997/04_97/diabetes.htm.

Mendosa, David. "David Mendosa: A Writer on the Web." Available online. URL: http://www.mendosa.com/index.html.

Morrison, Deane. "Defeating Diabetes: Across the University, the Battle Has Been Joined Against the Debilitating Disease," UMNnews Web site. Available online. URL: http://www1.umn.edu/umnnews/Feature_Stories/Defeating_diabetes.html.

"Our Goals," Juvenile Diabetes Research Foundation. Available online. URL: http://www.jdrf.org.uk/page.asp?section=0001000100050001&itemTitle=Our+goals.

"Patti LaBelle Kicking Diabetes 'In the Butt,'" October 28, 2004, NBC 10.com, Philadelphia Web site. Available online. URL: http://www.nbc10.com/health/3871037/detail.html.

The Pima Indians: Pathfinders for Health, "A Mother and Her Daughters," NIDDK Web site. Available online. URL: http://diabetes.niddk.nih.gov/dm/pubs/pima/mother/mother.htm.

Paracchini, Valentina, Paola Pedotti and Emanuela Taioli. "Genetics of Leptin and Obesity: A HuGE Review," *American Journal of Epidemiology* 162 (2005): 101–114. Available online. URL: http://aje.oxfordjournals.org/cgi/reprint/162/2/101.

Parson, Ann B. *The Proteus Effect: Stem Cells and Their Promise for Medicine.* Washington, DC: Joseph Henry Press, 2004.

Patlak, Margie. "New Weapons to Combat an Ancient Disease: Treating Diabetes," *FASEB Journal*, 2002. Available online. URL: http://www.fasebj.org/cgi/content/full/16/14/1853e.

Quick, William W., MD, FACP, FACE. "New to Diabetes?" The Diabetes Monitor Web site. Available online. URL: http://www.diabetesmonitor.com/new2dm.htm.

Quick, William W., MD, FACP, FACE, and Stephanie Schwartz Quick, RN, MPH, CDE. "Use of a Moderated Discussion Forum on the Internet for Patients to Share Experiences with New Diabetes Medications," The Diabetes Monitor Web site. Available online. URL: http://diabetes.blog.com/697635/.

Ridley, Matt. *Nature Via Nurture: Genes, Experience, and What Makes Us Human.* New York: HarperCollins, 2003.

Ruben, Alan L., MD. *Diabetes for Dummies.* 2nd ed. Hoboken, NJ.: Wiley Publishing, 2004.

Sanders, Lee J., DPM. "From Thebes to Toronto and the 21st Century: An Incredible Journey," *Diabetes Spectrum*, 15 (2002): 56–60, transcript of address at 2001 American Diabetes Association. Available online. URL: http://spectrum.diabetesjournals.org/cgi/content/full/15/1/56.

"Scientists Make Major Finding on Potential Cure for Type 1 Diabetes," April 23, 2006, *ScienceDaily* Web site. Available online. URL: http://www.sciencedaily.com/releases/2006/04/060423192408.htm.

Semple, Carol McCormick. *Diabetes: Revised Edition (Health Watch).* Berkeley Heights, NJ.: Enslow, 2000.

Siegler, Bonnie. "Halle Berry: My Battle with Diabetes," *Daily Mail*, December 14, 2005. Available online. URL: http://www.dailymail.co.uk/pages/live/articles/health/healthmain.html?in_article_id=371528&in_page_id=1774.

Snyder, Aaron. "Lifestyle Controls Rare Diabetes," Ripped: Success Stories. Available online. URL: http://www.cbass.com/success_stories8.htm.

Solomon, Nancy. "New Diabetes Research: Half of Americans Have Gene That Affects How Body Burns Sugar," St. Louis University, Eureka Alerts, Jan. 26, 2007. Available online. URL: http://www.eurekalert.org/pub_releases/2007-01/slu-ndr012607.php.

Somers, Terri. "Investors Wanted–Must Have Vision, Passion," December 17, 2006. SignOnSanDiego.com. Available online. URL: http://www.signonsandiego.com/uniontrib/20061217/news_mz1b17somers.html.

Stark, Jill. "Diabetes 'Threatens to Wipe Out Aborigines,'" The Age.com.au, November 13, 2006. Available online. URL: http://www.theage.com.au/news/national/diabetes-could-wipe-out-aborigines/2006/11/12/1163266413553.html.

Sullivan, Meg. "UCLA Study Finds Clues to Diabetes Puzzle," innovations report, 05.06.03. Available online. URL: http://innovations-report.com/html/reports/medicine_health/report-18969.html.

"TrialNet Project." DIPP–TEDDY–TRIALNET. Available online. URL: http://research.utu.fi/dipp/index.php?page=RESEARCHPROJ:TRIALNET&lang=EN&city=TURKU.

Trivedi, Bijal P. "Gene Therapy Succeeds in Mouse and Rat Models of Diabetes," November 27, 2001, Genome News Network. Available online. URL: http://www.genomenews-network.org/articles/11_00/therapy_diabetes.shtml.

"Type 1 Diabetes: From the Search for Causes to Studies on Prevention," Roche Web site. URL: http://www.roche.com/pages/downloads/science/pdf/rtdcmannh02-2.pdf.

University of Kentucky public relations, "Franklin County Boy to Be Featured During Annual Children's Miracle Network Celebration to Benefit Kentucky Children's Hospital," June 15, 2006, UK Health and Medical Science News. Available online.URL:http://www.uky.edu/PR/News/CMN/2006CMN-Franklin_County_Boy.htm.

University of Pittsburgh Medical Center press release, "Gene Therapy Technique Could Aid Islet Transplants for Diabetes, says Pittsburgh Study," May 2, 2004, accessed at Bio.com. Available online. URL: http://www.bio.com/newsfeatures/newsfeatures_research.jhtml?cid=132009796&page=1.

Watson, James D., with Andrew Berry. *DNA: The Secret of Life.* New York: Alfred A. Knopf, 2004.

"What is TEDDY?" TEDDY Web site. Available online. URL: http://teddy.epi.usf.edu/TEDDY/index.htm.

Wheelwright, Jeff. "Native America's Alleles," *Discover Magazine*, 26 (2005). Available online. URL: http://www.discover.com/issues/may-05/features/native-americas-alleles/?page=1.

FURTHER READING

Allan, Tony. *Understanding DNA: A Breakthrough in Medicine (Point of Impact)*. Chicago: Heinemann, 2002.

Alvin, Virginia and Silverstein, Robert. *Diabetes (Diseases and People)*. Springfield, N.J.: Enslow, 1994.

Fridell, Ron. *Genetic Engineering (Cool Science)*. Minneapolis: Lerner Publishing, 2005.

Hawkes, Chris. *The Human Body: Uncovering Science (Uncovering series)*. Tonawanda, N.Y.: Firefly Books, 2006.

Johnson, Rebecca L. *Genetics (Great Ideas in Science)*. Minneapolis: Lerner Publishing, 2005.

Moran, Katherine J. *Diabetes: The Ultimate Teen Guide (It Happened to Me)*. Lanham, MD: The Scarecrow Press, 2006.

Panno, Joseph, PhD. *Gene Therapy: Treating Disease by Repairing Genes (New Biology)*. New York: Facts on File, 2004.

Sheen, Barbara. *Diabetes (Diseases and Disorders)*. San Diego: Lucent Books, 2003.

Yuwiler, Janice M. *Insulin (Great Medical Discoveries)*. San Diego: Lucent, 2005.

WEB SITES

American Diabetes Association (http://www.diabetes.org/home.jsp).

Children with Diabetes (http://www.childrenwithdiabetes.com/index_cwd.htm).

Genetic Health: Diabetes (http://www.genetichealth.com/Diabetes_Home.shtml).

Genetics and Ethics (http://genethics.ca/).

The Human Genome (http://genome.wellcome.ac.uk/).

Joslin Diabetes Center (http://www.joslin.org/).

Juvenile Diabetes Research Foundation International (http://www.jdrf.org/).

Stem Cell Research Foundation (http://www.stemcellresearch-foundation.org/).

PICTURE CREDITS

INDEX

ABOUT THE AUTHOR

Toney Allman holds a B.S. from Ohio State University and an M.A. in clinical psychology from the University of Hawaii. She currently lives in rural Virginia. She has a special interest in science writing and research and has written more than two dozen nonfiction books for students. She has a longstanding interest in diabetes, since, like most Americans today, she has friends and family who cope with the disease.